FAMOUS BRIDGE DISASTERS

In this vastly entertaining book David Bird describes the most spectacular and amusing disasters suffered by the world's top players. There are two compelling reasons for studying such disasters – you can learn from them and (yes!) you can enjoy them.

In common with the previous books in this mini-series, you will be directly involved in the action at various stages, invited to make your own choice of bid, lead or play. This is excitement in itself for the hands are taken from top-class matches. You will be competing at world championship level.

Here is a wonderful chance to laugh, sympathise and learn under David Bird's expert guidance.

by DAVID BIRD

in the Master Bridge Series

with Terence Reese

Famous Bidding Decisions
Famous Play Decisions
Famous Leads and Defences
All You Need to Know about Play

The Monastery Books

Miracles of Card Play
Unholy Tricks: *More Miraculous Card Play*
Doubled and Venerable: *Further Miracles of Card Play*
Cardinal Sins
Divine Intervention
The Abbot and the Sensational Squeeze
* * *
with Ron Klinger
Kosher Bridge
Kosher Bridge 2
The Rabbi's Magic Trick: *More Kosher Bridge*
* * *
with Simon Cochemé
Bachelor Bridge: *the Amorous Adventures of Jack O'Hearts*
Bridge with a Feminine Touch

FAMOUS BRIDGE DISASTERS

David Bird

VICTOR GOLLANCZ
in association with
PETER CRAWLEY

First published in Great Britain 1999
in association with Peter Crawley
by Victor Gollancz
An imprint of the Orion Group
Orion House, 5 Upper Saint Martin's Lane, London WC2H 9EA

A catalogue record for this book
is available from the British Library

ISBN 0 575 06745 4

Typeset at The Spartan Press Ltd, Lymington, Hants
Printed in Great Britain by
Clays Ltd, St Ives plc.

Contents

Foreword

What is the purpose of a book portraying the most spectacular disasters suffered by the world's top players? There is a certain pleasure in seeing the mighty fall. No point in denying that, with TV 'out-take' programmes so high in the ratings. There is a grander purpose, however. By analysing how and why the various disasters occurred, we can hope to avoid such misfortune ourselves. What happens when a snooker professional misses a fairly easy blue into the middle pocket? He stares at the table for a second or two, fixing the error in his mind. The blue will drop next time, you can be sure. It's the same with bridge. By taking the time to analyse bad results, you can reduce the number of mistakes you make.

All the deals in this book come from the top level of play, mainly from world championships. The players named in the text have enjoyed countless triumphs and I trust they will not mind a spotlight being shone on their rare disasters. It is not our purpose to laugh at their discomfiture (except where it's unavoidable), more to draw instruction from the hands and improve our own standard of play.

My colleague in the research for this book has been, once again, Nikos Sarantakos. He is the one who has sent emails across the globe, asking such as 'Why on earth did the Ukrainian East double 4♡ on hand 29?' I am indebted also to David Gostyn, who has checked the manuscript and made many valuable suggestions.

David Bird

1. Disastrous Doubles

The opponents reach a freely-bid game and you can tell that the cards
lie badly for them. Are you tempted to double? There are many good
penalties to be reaped in this area and the Italian West player thought
the right moment had come, on this deal played against Ireland in the
1980 Olympiad at Valkenburg:

Game all
Dealer East

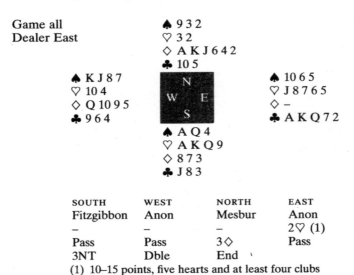

```
             ♠ 9 3 2
             ♡ 3 2
             ◇ A K J 6 4 2
             ♣ 10 5
♠ K J 8 7                      ♠ 10 6 5
♡ 10 4                         ♡ J 8 7 6 5
◇ Q 10 9 5                     ◇ –
♣ 9 6 4                        ♣ A K Q 7 2
             ♠ A Q 4
             ♡ A K Q 9
             ◇ 8 7 3
             ♣ J 8 3
```

SOUTH	WEST	NORTH	EAST
Fitzgibbon	Anon	Mesbur	Anon
–	–	–	2♡ (1)
Pass	Pass	3◇	Pass
3NT	Dble	End	

(1) 10–15 points, five hearts and at least four clubs

It will be normal practice in this book to name all the participants.
However, at final proof stage a cheque arrived with an impressive
number of zeros on the amount. Reluctantly, I agreed to withhold the
names of the Italians sitting East–West.

West had the spades and diamonds under control and his partner
had shown the other two suits. He therefore deemed it right to double
3NT. Had he backed this with a club lead, his judgement would have
been vindicated. His actual choice was a less effective ♡10. Fitzgibbon
won and advanced ◇8. Put yourself in the West seat. Would you have
covered this card?

West covered with the 9 and declarer called for dummy's jack, East
showing out. A finesse of ♡9 succeeded and declarer continued with
◇7, covered by the 10 and king. A spade to the ace allowed declarer to

cash the good hearts and take the marked finesse of dummy's ◇ 6. Two doubled overtricks resulted, giving the Irish a score of +1150.

Had the Italian West not doubled 3NT, he could have played low on ◇ 8 without a care. There would be no reason to expect the card to be run. After West's double, however, declarer had every reason to place him with all four diamonds (why double with just ◇ Q 10 5 under the bid suit?). With a fair expectation that ◇ 8 would be run, it was understandable that West covered. At least this would prevent the horror of the suit being run when South held only two diamonds.

Right, I must take this cheque to the bank. Wait a minute, I thought it was made out in US dollars but it's only Italian lire! In that case the amount is not nearly enough. No, journalistic integrity *must* prevail. Benito Garozzo was the West player, partnering Lorenzo Lauria.

Great Britain faced Austria on the next deal, from the 1989 European Championships in Turku, Finland. What do you make of East's penalty double of 4♠?

North–South game
Dealer South

```
                    ♠ A Q 6 3 2
                    ♡ 7 6 5 4
                    ◇ 6
                    ♣ 10 8 6
   ♠ 10 4              N              ♠ K
   ♡ A J 9 8 3                        ♡ K Q 10 2
   ◇ 10 8 7 3     W       E           ◇ J 9 5 2
   ♣ 9 5                              ♣ K Q J 3
                    S
                    ♠ J 9 8 7 5
                    ♡ –
                    ◇ A K Q 4
                    ♣ A 7 4 2
```

SOUTH	WEST	NORTH	EAST
Forrester	Fucik	Brock	Kubak
1♠	Pass	3♠	Dble
Pass	4♡	Pass	Pass
4♠	Pass	Pass	Dble
End			

Forrester ruffed the heart lead and played a trump to the ace. The king fell offside and he then made all thirteen tricks on a cross-ruff. That was +1390, almost as much as he would have scored for bidding the small slam.

It was smart of Forrester to pass initially over East's double and Kubak must have assumed that the subsequent 4♠ was a sacrifice. The final double was poor, nevertheless. Kubak had limited defence in his own hand and if his partner held a couple of defensive tricks he would have doubled himself.

Good players are always alert for the chance to make a lead-directing double of an artificial bid, such as a Blackwood response, a cue bid, or a fourth-suit-forcing call. I had an unlucky experience in this area myself once, playing in the Cino del Duca pairs in Paris. The opponents started their bidding: $1\diamond - 2\clubsuit - 2\spadesuit - 3\heartsuit$. On a hand including $\heartsuit$A K 10 5 2 and not much else I was not slow to double the fourth-suit call. Unknown to me, it was not a fourth-suit call. It was a canapé sequence showing a strong responding hand with good hearts! The next player promptly redoubled and ten tricks were made.

Even world champions can get their fingers burned with this type of double. Eric Rodwell sat West on the next deal, facing Omar Sharif and Zia in the 1995 Macallan Pairs.

Game all
Dealer South

	♠ J 6 5	
	♡ A K 5	
	◇ A 10 9 7 2	
	♣ A K	
♠ K 4 3 2	N	♠ A Q 8 7
♡ 9	W E	♡ Q 6 3 2
◇ Q J 8 6 5	S	◇ –
♣ J 7 2		♣ 10 9 8 4 3
	♠ 10 9	
	♡ J 10 8 7 4	
	◇ K 4 3	
	♣ Q 6 5	

SOUTH	WEST	NORTH	EAST
Sharif	Rodwell	Zia	Meckstroth
Pass	Pass	2NT	Pass
3◇	Dble	Rdble	End

Zia's redouble showed a good diamond holding. Sharif, who could add $\diamond$K x x to the pot, was happy to pass. Rodwell led a club to dummy's ace and Sharif played a spade, preparing for a ruff in that suit. West won and the defenders played two more rounds of spades. Sharif ruffed the third round and played a heart to the ace. He then cashed dummy's second club honour, played a trump to the king, and threw dummy's heart loser on the club queen. Now came a trump through West's holding. The defenders could score only two spades and two trumps, giving North–South an unusual +840. At the other tables game in hearts or no-trumps was defeated by the bad breaks.

Do you play Lightner Doubles? Of course you do. It was a brilliant invention by Theodore Lightner and one of the world's most widely played conventions. You may be surprised to hear that Terence Reese once expressed doubt that the Lightner Double had shown a net profit over its long lifetime. One big risk is that the opponents may run to a safer spot. That's what happened when China faced the Central American team on this deal from the 1979 Bermuda Bowl in Rio:

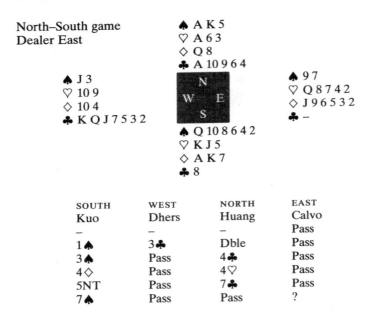

North–South game
Dealer East

North
♠ A K 5
♡ A 6 3
♢ Q 8
♣ A 10 9 6 4

West
♠ J 3
♡ 10 9
♢ 10 4
♣ K Q J 7 5 3 2

East
♠ 9 7
♡ Q 8 7 4 2
♢ J 9 6 5 3 2
♣ —

South
♠ Q 10 8 6 4 2
♡ K J 5
♢ A K 7
♣ 8

SOUTH	WEST	NORTH	EAST
Kuo	Dhers	Huang	Calvo
–	–	–	Pass
1♠	3♣	Dble	Pass
3♠	Pass	4♣	Pass
4♢	Pass	4♡	Pass
5NT	Pass	7♣	Pass
7♠	Pass	Pass	?

Would you have made a Lightner Double on the East cards? There are two reasons why it may not be a good idea. Firstly, is it clear that the double would request a club lead? Many players have a rule that a Lightner Double specifically excludes the lead of any suit bid by the partnership. Secondly, a double might allow the opponents to run to 7NT.

Calvo did double and Patrick Huang, sitting North, had no difficulty in reading the situation. He corrected to 7NT and this was easily made with the aid of a heart finesse. At the other table the contract was Six Spades, so the Central American team lost 13 IMPs where they might have gained 18.

When the same deal arose in another match, USA's Paul Soloway held the East cards. He doubled an earlier club bid (a cue-bid of 5♣) but did not double the final contract of Seven Spades. A club ruff put the contract one down. Calvo might have followed similar tactics, doubling the 4♣ cue-bid.

When the Lightner Double is employed against a small slam a different problem may arise. After the suggested ruff is scored, there may be no second trick to take. Occasionally the slam succeeds after the ruff, but might have gone down without it. That happened when Poland faced USA in the 1988 Olympiad:

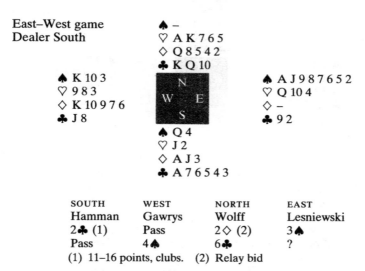

East–West game
Dealer South

```
                    ♠ –
                    ♡ A K 7 6 5
                    ◇ Q 8 5 4 2
                    ♣ K Q 10
    ♠ K 10 3                           ♠ A J 9 8 7 6 5 2
    ♡ 9 8 3                            ♡ Q 10 4
    ◇ K 10 9 7 6                       ◇ –
    ♣ J 8                              ♣ 9 2
                    ♠ Q 4
                    ♡ J 2
                    ◇ A J 3
                    ♣ A 7 6 5 4 3
```

SOUTH	WEST	NORTH	EAST
Hamman	Gawrys	Wolff	Lesniewski
2♣ (1)	Pass	2◇ (2)	3♠
Pass	4♠	6♣	?

(1) 11–16 points, clubs. (2) Relay bid.

Would you have made a Lightner Double on the East cards? Lesniewski did and a diamond lead duly materialised. It was the only trick the Poles made. Declarer drew trumps and set up dummy's heart suit to dispose of his remaining losers. Exactly the same thing happened at the other table. Balicki made Six Clubs doubled and both sides recorded +1090.

Big deal, you may be saying. If East doesn't double, he picks up 5 IMPs for −920 against the other room's −1090. Perhaps it would have been very much more! McKinnon, for the Australian women's team, played in Six Clubs undoubled. She ruffed the spade lead and drew one round of trumps with the king. Not forewarned by a Lightner Double, she then called for a diamond. East ruffed and returned the spade ace, forcing dummy to ruff and killing the entry to the potential long cards in hearts. With nowhere to hide her diamond loser, declarer went one down.

Most doubles of no-trump contracts from 3NT upwards are played as lead-directing. One such double misfired in the 1990 World Pairs final.

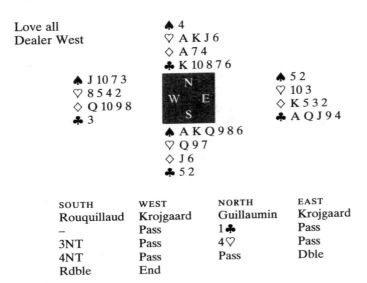

Love all
Dealer West

		♠ 4	
		♡ A K J 6	
		◇ A 7 4	
		♣ K 10 8 7 6	

♠ J 10 7 3		♠ 5 2
♡ 8 5 4 2		♡ 10 3
◇ Q 10 9 8		◇ K 5 3 2
♣ 3		♣ A Q J 9 4

		♠ A K Q 9 8 6	
		♡ Q 9 7	
		◇ J 6	
		♣ 5 2	

SOUTH	WEST	NORTH	EAST
Rouquillaud	Krojgaard	Guillaumin	Krojgaard
–	Pass	1♣	Pass
3NT	Pass	4♡	Pass
4NT	Pass	Pass	Dble
Rdble	End		

Most pairs played in 4♠, scoring below average (41%) for their 420s. Rouquillaud of France shot for a top, responding 3NT on the South cards. His partner (who had clearly not caught a glimpse of the East hand) visualised a club slam. He made a natural slam try of 4♡ and passed the sign-off in 4NT. Suppose this had been passed out. Would West have led a spade, letting the contract make, or a diamond for two down? We will never know. East doubled, for a club lead, and a club was duly led to dummy's 10 and East's jack. No immediate damage had been done, but what should East do next? A diamond switch scarcely looked attractive from his side of the table.

Puzzled that no-one had bid spades, East switched to ♠5 at trick 2. Declarer took the three top spades, East showing out on the third round. When the spade suit was cleared, poor West had no further club to lead. Declarer made the contract exactly, finding a novel route to +920.

Sometimes the opponents have a bidding misunderstanding and end up playing in a ludicrous fit at a high level. Even at world championship level there are examples of a defender foolishly doubling in the pass-out seat, allowing the opponents to jump back into their big fit. Here's a spectacular example from the quarter-finals of the 1984 Olympiad, with Poland facing Pakistan.

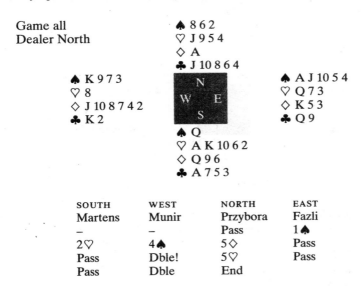

Game all
Dealer North

```
                    ♠ 8 6 2
                    ♡ J 9 5 4
                    ◇ A
                    ♣ J 10 8 6 4
♠ K 9 7 3                              ♠ A J 10 5 4
♡ 8              N                     ♡ Q 7 3
◇ J 10 8 7 4 2   W    E                ◇ K 5 3
♣ K 2              S                   ♣ Q 9
                    ♠ Q
                    ♡ A K 10 6 2
                    ◇ Q 9 6
                    ♣ A 7 5 3
```

SOUTH	WEST	NORTH	EAST
Martens	Munir	Przybora	Fazli
–	–	Pass	1♠
2♡	4♠	5◇	Pass
Pass	Dble!	5♡	Pass
Pass	Dble	End	

Since Przybora was a passed hand, he felt that his 5◇ bid would be unambiguously lead-directing. He explained it as such to his screen-mate, Fazli. The two players on the other side of the screen were not in on the secret. Martens passed and Munir had only to pass to collect at least 600. No, he felt impelled to double 5◇. Imagine the look that Przybora and Fazli must have exchanged as the bidding tray reappeared under the screen! Przybora rescued himself to 5♡ and Munir felt obliged to double that contract too.

How much did Munir's indiscretion cost him, do you think? It was one of the least expensive bidding 'disasters' on record. After West's double of 5♡ Martens played for the drop in trumps and went one down for −200. At the other table (after bidding of 1♠ − 2♡ − 4♠ − 5♡, Dble) Zia guessed the trumps correctly to record +850. So the Pakistanis gained 14 IMPs anyway.

I have two strong contenders for the 'most disastrous double ever' award and will leave you to choose between them. The first arose in the final of the 1989 Venice Cup in Perth, with USA facing the Netherlands.

North–South game
Dealer East

```
              ♠ –
              ♡ A 7
              ◇ K 5 2
              ♣ A K Q 8 6 5 4 3
♠ 10 9 4                         ♠ K 8 7 6 5 2
♡ K 9 8 6 5 4        N           ♡ J
◇ 8 4             W     E        ◇ Q J 10 6
♣ 9 2                S           ♣ 10 7
              ♠ A Q J 3
              ♡ Q 10 3 2
              ◇ A 9 7 3
              ♣ J
```

SOUTH	WEST	NORTH	EAST
Gielkens	Bethe	Bakker	Gwozdzinsky
–	–	–	2♠ (1)
2NT	3♠	4♠	Pass
5♡	Pass	7♣	Pass
7◇	Pass	Pass	Dble!
7NT	Dble	End	

(1) Weak two, 6–10 points

If Bakker was intending to bid 7♣, come what may, it was a poor idea to preface it with 4♠. Gielkens was entitled to assume that her partner held a two-suiter, correcting the contract to 7◇ as a result.

The Dutch North passed, doubtless not too happy with this turn of events. Gwozdzinsky, East for USA, took a look at her impressive trump holding and doubled 7◇. She was not particularly worried when the opponents ran to 7NT, doubled by West. Not, that is, until dummy went down with an 8-card club suit! West gave nothing away with her diamond lead but Gielkens made thirteen tricks by squeezing East in spades and diamonds.

At the other table the USA North scored 1390 in Six Clubs. The Americans therefore lost 15 IMPs when they could have gained 17 IMPs by defending the diamond grand.

How much was Gwozdzinsky to blame? Of course it was unlucky to find that 7NT was a make. The main point to remember is that a slam double that turns 50 into 100, or 100 into 200, may gain not a single IMP when the contract is different at the other table. Suppose you double a grand slam, beating it by one, and your team-mates make a small slam: 920+100 is worth 15 IMPs, the same as 920+50. If the opponents are vulnerable, 1430+100 is worth 17 IMPs, the same as 1430+200. It's the same when you double a small slam, one down, and your team-mates play in game: 100+450 is worth 11 IMPs, the same as 50+450; 200+650 is worth 13 IMPs, the same as 100+650. Not a single IMP is gained by such doubles. And when a slam double mis-fires, as here, the cost can be 32 IMPs!

I know what you're thinking: that double of 7◇ MUST have been the most disastrous double ever. No, I rate the next one as a worthy rival. Sweden faced Germany in the 1997 European Championships in Montecatini.

Love all
Dealer North

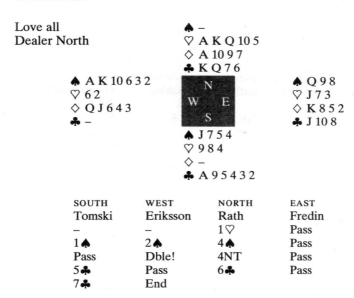

```
                    ♠ –
                    ♡ A K Q 10 5
                    ◇ A 10 9 7
                    ♣ K Q 7 6
  ♠ A K 10 6 3 2                      ♠ Q 9 8
  ♡ 6 2                               ♡ J 7 3
  ◇ Q J 6 4 3                         ◇ K 8 5 2
  ♣ –                                 ♣ J 10 8
                    ♠ J 7 5 4
                    ♡ 9 8 4
                    ◇ –
                    ♣ A 9 5 4 3 2
```

SOUTH	WEST	NORTH	EAST
Tomski	Eriksson	Rath	Fredin
–	–	1♡	Pass
1♠	2♠	4♠	Pass
Pass	Dble!	4NT	Pass
5♣	Pass	6♣	Pass
7♣	End		

West's 2♠ was natural, a common interpretation nowadays. Since Rath would have doubled, holding spades, he somewhat eccentrically bid 4♠ to show a massive three-suiter outside spades. A puzzled Tomski eventually passed, leaving his side in a 4–0 fit.

The Swedish cavalry now arrived. Eriksson administered a penalty double! The German North wisely decided not to rely on his partner to remove the double. He pulled to 4NT and, when partner showed a club suit, raised him to the slam. Realising now that North must be void in spades, South bid a seventh club. The contract proved unbeatable. Having missed the chance to defend Four Spades, the Swedes were doubtless reluctant to sacrifice in Seven Spades on their own cards.

This was the bidding at the other table:

SOUTH	WEST	NORTH	EAST
Fallenius	Holowski	Nilsland	Gotard
–	–	1 ♡	Pass
2 ♡	4 ♠	Pass	Pass
Dble	End		

Surely North could venture 5 ♡ on his 3-loser hand? It takes a club lead to beat *Seven* Hearts! Adding insult to injury, the Swedes failed to take any diamond ruffs in defence. North discarded a diamond when the trumps were drawn, destroying his second diamond trick, and the spade game was made. That was a further 590 to Germany and a swing of 19 IMPs.

2. Disasters in Cashing Out

Sometimes a contract can be beaten in top cards, either at the time of the opening lead or subsequently. It is not always easy for the defenders to find their tricks and in this chapter we will look at some spectacular failures to do so. As always, our aim will be two-fold: to have a quiet chuckle at the disasters the great stars encountered, and to ensure that we avoid similar accidents ourselves.

We begin with the classic situation where the defenders have two aces to cash against a small slam. The 1973 Bermuda Bowl was played on the island of Guaruja, an exclusive Brazilian resort. (There's a saying in Brazil: the rich take their holidays in Europe, the very rich in Guaruja.) A vociferous VuGraph audience was backing the home team against North America.

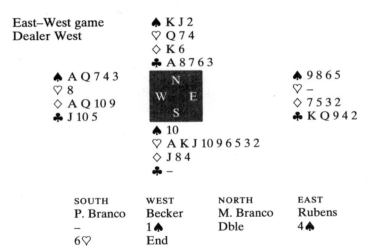

East–West game   ♠ K J 2
Dealer West   ♡ Q 7 4
    ◇ K 6
    ♣ A 8 7 6 3

♠ A Q 7 4 3   ♠ 9 8 6 5
♡ 8   ♡ –
◇ A Q 10 9   ◇ 7 5 3 2
♣ J 10 5   ♣ K Q 9 4 2

    ♠ 10
    ♡ A K J 10 9 6 5 3 2
    ◇ J 8 4
    ♣ –

SOUTH	WEST	NORTH	EAST
P. Branco	Becker	M. Branco	Rubens
–	1♠	Dble	4♠
6♡	End		

Pedro Branco was looking for particular cards from partner when he ventured 6♡. Mind you, it's not often that you hold 9-card support for the unbid major. Becker led the ace of diamonds and surveyed the dummy. His partner had made a vulnerable leap to 4♠ on very few values. He was likely to hold five spades, which would leave South with a void. Indeed the very fact that South had leapt to six, on a hand with only one ace, strongly suggested that he was void in spades. Reasoning in this way, Becker switched to ♣J at trick 2. Cheers erupted from the home VuGraph crowd. Branco discarded his spade loser and claimed 12 tricks with the aid of a diamond ruff.

Time for our assessment. How much was Becker to blame? The odds were certainly high that declarer was void in spades. The question is: if the ace of spades were to be ruffed, would one discard on the spade king be critical? Declarer could ruff any diamond losers, so only a club discard would be useful. Allowing declarer to ruff a switch to ♠A would cost the contract if South held a hand such as:

♠ —		♠ —
♡ A K J 10 9 6 5 3	or	♡ A K J 10 9 6 5 3
◇ J 8 4		◇ J 8
♣ Q 4		♣ K 9 4

These are quite possible holdings for South, particularly the one on the right. I don't think we should blame Becker too much for his club switch.

Using the signalling methods of today, East could have assisted his partner. With no further trick available in diamonds, most defenders would signal suit preference on partner's diamond ace. Here East would signal with his highest spot-card, the 7, to suggest that West cashes the spade ace. If West held six spades rather than five he would ignore the suggestion, knowing anyway that declarer was void.

The disaster might be avoided in quite a different way – during the auction! In the sequence 1♠ – Dble – 4♣, the 4♣ response is widely played nowadays as a fit-jump rather than a splinter bid. It would show a game raise in spades, including a good side suit of clubs. Had East made such a response West could fearlessly switch to the spade ace at trick 2. Since declarer could hold at most one club, he would have no useful discard on the spade king.

Perhaps we can find someone to blame on the next hand, from the final of the 1976 Bermuda Bowl between USA and Italy.

East–West game
Dealer North

```
                    ♠ A K Q 7 2
                    ♡ 8 6 3
                    ◇ J 9 7
                    ♣ J 3
    ♠ 6 5                           ♠ 9
    ♡ A J 10 7          N           ♡ K Q 9 2
    ◇ 10 8 6 3      W       E       ◇ Q 5 4 2
    ♣ 10 4 2            S           ♣ A K 8 7
                    ♠ J 10 8 4 3
                    ♡ 5 4
                    ◇ A K
                    ♣ Q 9 6 5
```

SOUTH	WEST	NORTH	EAST
Garozzo	Ross	Franco	Paulsen
–	–	Pass	1♡
1♠	2♡	4♠	Dble
End			

The auction was exactly the same at both tables, although I'm slightly surprised at the final double found by the two East players. Suppose you had been West. What would you have led?

At the other table the Italian West saw no reason not to lead the ace of hearts and the defenders soon had four tricks in the bag. Ross feared that the heart king might be on his right and looked elsewhere, trying ◇3. 'Nine, please,' said the declarer and all now depended on East's action. When he contributed the queen declarer had a discard for one of his losing hearts. +590 and 12 IMPs to the Italians.

Could the disaster have been avoided? West might perhaps have led ◇8, making it clear that he was seeking an entry to his partner's hand (for a heart switch), rather than trying to set up tricks in diamonds. After the actual ◇3 lead, was East right to contribute the queen to the first trick? He could guess from West's failure to lead a heart that West held the heart ace. If West held ◇K as well, this would leave only an ace, a queen and two jacks to make up South's overcall.

Another strong pointer in the winning direction is that it will not necessarily be fatal to withhold the queen when partner has led from the king. Unless declarer started with only one heart, which is unlikely after West's single raise, he will still have four losers (♡A K ♣A K).

There was an element of comedy on the next deal, from the 1988 Olympiad. Despite an inordinately long relay sequence, not worthy of our inspection, Miyakuni of Japan reached 6NT with two aces missing.

Game all

Dealer South

```
                    ♠ 3 2
                    ♡ K J 5
                    ◇ Q 3
                    ♣ Q J 9 7 5 4
    ♠ 7 6 5 4              N          ♠ A J 10
    ♡ Q 9 3 2                         ♡ 10 8 4
    ◇ 6 4           W        E        ◇ 10 9 8 7 2
    ♣ A 6 2              S            ♣ 10 8
                    ♠ K Q 9 8
                    ♡ A 7 6
                    ◇ A K J 5
                    ♣ K 3
```

During the auction North had described his hand with a series of relay responses. Little was known of the South hand, except that it was strong. Having been informed that dummy would contain a 6-card club suit, Coenraets (West for Belgium) made an attacking lead in hearts, rather than the normally recommended safe lead against 6NT. Miyakuni inserted ♡J successfully, then played a club to the king.

Suppose West were to win with the ace. He would then have to guess whether to play a spade or a diamond. Hoping for a helpful discard from his partner, the Belgian West ducked the first round of clubs. South now led a second round of clubs. If West won this trick and his partner followed suit again, he would still have to make the key decision without the assistance of a discard. Coenraets therefore held off the second club too.

The Japanese declarer knew that his chance of making the contract was zero if he played another club. West would win and East would throw a big spade, or a low diamond, telling West what to do. He therefore switched his attention to spades, hoping for some miracle in that suit. His prayers were answered! East held A J 10 bare – South's holding was worth three tricks. +1440.

How might East–West have done better? With a certain ♡K entry to the dummy, there was little value to a count signal in clubs. Some defenders would therefore attach suit-preference connotations to East's plays in the club suit. The 10 followed by the 8 would suggest West switched to spades rather than diamonds.

Moving relentlessly forward, we reach the 1998 Cavendish International Pairs in Las Vegas. In this popular form of tournament, each of the pairs is auctioned before the play starts. Large sums of money go to the players who finish in the first few places, and to those who bought them in the auction. On this occasion the total pool was a record, in excess of one million dollars! Any disaster was likely to prove expensive.

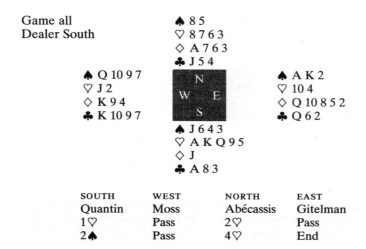

Game all
Dealer South

	♠ 8 5	
	♡ 8 7 6 3	
	◇ A 7 6 3	
	♣ J 5 4	

♠ Q 10 9 7		♠ A K 2
♡ J 2	N	♡ 10 4
◇ K 9 4	W E	◇ Q 10 8 5 2
♣ K 10 9 7	S	♣ Q 6 2

	♠ J 6 4 3	
	♡ A K Q 9 5	
	◇ J	
	♣ A 8 3	

SOUTH	WEST	NORTH	EAST
Quantin	Moss	Abécassis	Gitelman
1♡	Pass	2♡	Pass
2♠	Pass	4♡	End

Quantin's 2♠ was long-suit game try. Abécassis held four trumps and a useful doubleton in the game-try suit. Even so, it was ambitious to accept the try on such slender values. Brad Moss led ♣10, taken by declarer's ace. Declarer drew one round of trumps, then led a low spade. The defenders seemed certain to score two tricks in each black suit. How did they go astray?

Brad Moss won the first round of spades with the 9. Knowing that his partner held the club queen, he continued with ♣7. He was aware of the club situation but his partner was not. Thinking that West had led from ♣10 9 8 7 and that declarer had started with ♣A K 3, Fred Gitelman allowed the 7 to run! Declarer won gratefully with the 8, gave up another spade, and subsequently scored two spade ruffs to land the game. When the result was cross-IMPed against all the other tables, the cost to East–West was a massive 297 IMPs.

The disaster could easily have been avoided. West should have continued with king and another club. Failing that, he should have led the 9 of clubs rather than the 7. The lesson of the hand is to visualise the problems that partner may have, even when the required defence is obvious from your side of the table.

On to the 1998 Cap Gemini World Top tournament. The Hackett twins from Great Britain finished fourth among a field of world champions despite a cash-out disaster on this deal:

Game all   ♠ 9 6
Dealer North   ♡ J 2
                 ◇ A J 10 9 7 4 2
                 ♣ 6 3

♠ A K 10 4 3		♠ J 8 2
♡ 10 7 5	N	♡ Q 8 4
◇ 3	W E	◇ 8 6 5
♣ Q J 8 7	S	♣ A K 9 4

                 ♠ Q 7 5
                 ♡ A K 9 6 3
                 ◇ K Q
                 ♣ 10 5 2

SOUTH	WEST	NORTH	EAST
Westra	Jason H	Leufkens	Justin H
–	–	3◇	Pass
3♡	Pass	4♡	End

There were two purposes to Westra's 3♡ response. It might deter
the opponents from bidding game in a black suit. Failing that, partner
would have a good idea what to lead. The opponents declined to enter
the auction, as it happened, and a few moments later Westra was
installed in 4♡.

Jason Hackett led ♠K, receiving a count signal of the 2. What now?
If partner could look after the diamond suit, it seemed that declarer
might bump his total to ten only by taking a black-suit ruff or two in
the dummy. Jason switched boldly to a trump and found this switch
doubly unlucky. Firstly, declarer's trumps were headed by A K 9 and
the switch actually cost a trump trick. Secondly, the diamonds were
ready to run! It was +680 to the Dutchmen and a costly upset for the
deadly duo.

Would you have done better from the West seat? Although the
trump switch led to a comical result, it seems to me that it was well
reasoned. There are various possible South hands where a trump
switch would have proved effective.

3. Disastrous Penalties

In this chapter we will look closely at some occasions where the world's top players have gone for a glaringly big number. There will be little serious point to such an exercise unless we can draw benefit from it, trying to analyse how the penalties might have been avoided or reduced.

What do you regard as the minimum standards for an opening bid at the one-level? Among some experts – Meckstroth and Rodwell, for example – it is the fashion nowadays to open on flat 11-counts. Even when vulnerable against not. To discover why this is a good idea you will have to buy some other book (you didn't *borrow* this masterpiece, did you?). Call me old-fashioned, but I neither understand nor condone such a practice. Advocates claim that it makes the opponents' bidding more difficult if your side is first to speak. I don't regard an opening of 1♣ or 1♢ as much of a hazard.

Look at the following hand, which actually has a point to spare – 12 points rather than 11:

♠ 4 3 2   ♡ K J 7 4   ♢ A 7 3   ♣ A 10 8

You are vulnerable against not, playing a strong no-trump and five-card majors. The player in front of you passes. Would you open 1♣ or make a cautious pass?

Norman Kay, a player renowned for avoiding risks, decided to open 1♣. It cost his team the 1971 Spingold Final! This was the deal:

North–South game
Dealer East

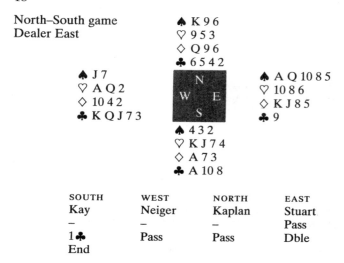

```
                    ♠ K 9 6
                    ♡ 9 5 3
                    ◇ Q 9 6
                    ♣ 6 5 4 2
      ♠ J 7                           ♠ A Q 10 8 5
      ♡ A Q 2            N            ♡ 10 8 6
      ◇ 10 4 2      W        E        ◇ K J 8 5
      ♣ K Q J 7 3        S            ♣ 9
                    ♠ 4 3 2
                    ♡ K J 7 4
                    ◇ A 7 3
                    ♣ A 10 8
```

SOUTH	WEST	NORTH	EAST
Kay	Neiger	Kaplan	Stuart
–	–	–	Pass
1♣	Pass	Pass	Dble
End			

Joel Stuart made the fine decision to re-open with a double, rather than 1♠. There was no further bidding and Neiger's lead of the trump king held declarer to just two tricks for a penalty of 1400. The final was a clash between experience (Mathe–Krauss, Kaplan–Kay) and a young Precision team. Unexpectedly, it was the younger player who declined to open on the South cards. His side gained 15 IMPs on the deal (Mathe making two overtricks in 2NT) and went on to win by just 7 IMPs.

Was it a mistake to open on those South cards? If you were playing a weak no-trump even when vulnerable, it's the sort of 9-loser hand on which you might decide to pass. The risk of a penalty is less when you can open 1♣, but I still question the *advantage* of opening, particularly when you are not naming a suit that you would like to be led.

Did you choose to pass on the South cards? If so, I congratulate you – either on your good judgement or your astuteness in recalling the title of this chapter.

What could be more disastrous than to rescue partner from a doubled contract that he would have made into an alternative spot where he goes 1400 down? It happened in the qualifying rounds of the 1991 World Championship, with Egypt facing USA.

Game all

Dealer East

```
                    ♠ A 4 3
                    ♡ 10 9 8 7 3
                    ◇ 7 3
                    ♣ 9 4 2
    ♠ 8 6 2              N           ♠ J 9 5
    ♡ A J 5 2       W        E       ♡ K Q 6
    ◇ 9 8                            ◇ A Q
    ♣ A J 5 3           S            ♣ K 10 8 7 6
                    ♠ K Q 10 7
                    ♡ 4
                    ◇ K J 10 6 5 4 2
                    ♣ Q
```

SOUTH	WEST	NORTH	EAST
Kordy	Rodwell	Salib	Meckstroth
–	–	–	1NT (1)
2♠ (2)	Dble (3)	3♣	Dble
3◇	3NT	Pass	Pass
4◇	Dble	Pass	Dble
End			

(1) 14–16 points   (2) Spades + minor   (3) Negative

South would have made his 4◇ doubled but the correction to 4♠ cost 1400. This was 20 IMPs to USA when a briefer auction at the other table (1NT – 3◇ – Dble) yielded them a further 870.

Why was North's correction wrong? His partner had made a vulnerable sacrifice in diamonds, knowing that the opponents held a clear balance of the points. Such a bid showed considerable playing strength in diamonds. It did not guarantee playing strength in spades. Indeed, a spade contract was likely to play very poorly with South holding only four spades. The diamonds would not be ready to run (or South would have defended 3NT) and declarer would doubtless be forced in hearts or clubs.

The situation North faced should not be confused with that when a player opens the bidding in one suit, then makes a high bid in a second suit. In that case responder does have a free choice between the suits. On the auction here South had shown excellent diamonds and only a side-suit of spades.

Kordy and Salib were not the only pair to end in the awful 4♠ contract. Polish stars, Gawrys and Lasocki, did the same. Fame has some advantages, though. The opponents declined to double and they went 'only' 500 down.

The next deal comes from the 1961 Master Pairs. Look first at the South hand. What would you have bid over East's pre-emptive 3◇ opening?

North–South game	♠ K Q 5 4		
Dealer East	♡ Q 6		
	◇ J 5		
	♣ 9 8 6 5 4		

♠ J 10 7 6		♠ 8 3
♡ A K J 7 2	N	♡ 3
◇ A 10 2	W E	◇ K Q 9 8 7 6 4 3
♣ 3	S	♣ 10 2

♠ A 9 2
♡ 10 9 8 5 4
◇ –
♣ A K Q J 7

SOUTH	WEST	NORTH	EAST
Hockwald	Rodrigue	Schapiro	Flint
–	–	–	3◇
3♡	Pass	4♡	Pass
Pass	Dble	End	

What was your choice on the South cards? I don't like 3♡ at all, on such a weak suit. Surely a take-out double is better and would have led to a safer spot in one of the black suits. Rodrigue showed excellent judgement in passing 3♡ but when Schapiro raised to 4♡ – a dubious move on those values – he thought it safe to double.

Hochwald ruffed the diamond lead, played a trump to West's king, and ruffed the diamond return. He now lost track completely, playing two rounds of clubs. Rodrigue ruffed and drew trumps, after which East could run his diamond suit. That was seven down and a penalty of 2000.

What lesson can we draw from this misfortune? When things go wrong on a hand, don't panic or play quickly in a desire to bring the horrible experience to an end. After ruffing the second diamond, declarer could have scored three spades and a spade ruff, before turning to clubs. This would have restricted the penalty to 800. Not that the match-pointer would have been unduly exerted.

Are you happy to open 1NT on a hand with a 5-card major? You are more likely to answer 'Yes' if you play a strong no-trump. That's because such hands may otherwise cause a rebid problem. Zia Mahmood regretted his decision to open 1NT on this deal from the 1998 Macallan Pairs:

Game all
Dealer South

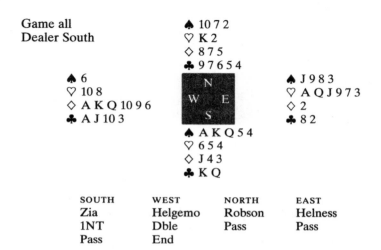

	♠ 10 7 2
	♡ K 2
	♢ 8 7 5
	♣ 9 7 6 5 4

♠ 6
♡ 10 8
♢ A K Q 10 9 6
♣ A J 10 3

♠ J 9 8 3
♡ A Q J 9 7 3
♢ 2
♣ 8 2

♠ A K Q 5 4
♡ 6 5 4
♢ J 4 3
♣ K Q

SOUTH	WEST	NORTH	EAST
Zia	Helgemo	Robson	Helness
1NT	Dble	Pass	Pass
Pass	End		

Zia opened a 15–17 point 1NT and Helgemo doubled for penalties.
Neither Robson nor Zia saw fit to retreat into a suit and the defenders
ran West's diamonds, followed by East's hearts. Prompted by a suit
preference indication on the last three diamond leads (6, 9, then 10),
Helness had kept a club with his hearts, rather than a spade. Zia scored
no tricks at all and went 2000 down!

Should North–South have avoided this outcome somehow? Zia
certainly had no reason to run after the double. He could expect his
spades to score tricks in no-trumps. Many players would have run to
2♣ on the North cards. This would still cost a fortune if West were
able to sink his teeth into it. East would surely bid in front of West,
however, letting the opponents off the hook. A player who doubles a
strong no-trump is more likely to have a long suit to run than someone
who doubles a weak no-trump. All in all, the odds perhaps favour a
retreat to 2♣ on the North cards.

Back in 1961 the French team visited Brazil to play some friendly
matches in preparation for the Bermuda Bowl of that year. It was well
past midnight when a deal arose that was to become known as the
'Earthquake of Sao Paolo'. This was it:

Game all   ♠ —
Dealer North   ♡ A Q 10 9 8 7 6 5 4 3 2
                 ♢ —
                 ♣ K 4

♠ K Q 10 6 5 4 3   ♠ A J 9 8 7 2
♡ —   ♡ —
♢ 7 6   ♢ 5 4 3 2
♣ J 10 8 6   ♣ 9 7 5

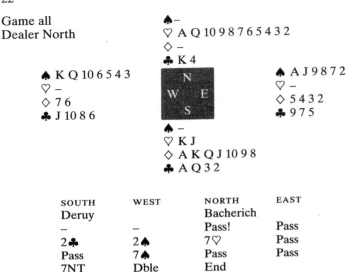

                 ♠ —
                 ♡ K J
                 ♢ A K Q J 10 9 8
                 ♣ A Q 3 2

SOUTH	WEST	NORTH	EAST
Deruy		Bacherich	
–	–	Pass!	Pass
2♣	2♠	7♡	Pass
Pass	7♠	Pass	Pass
7NT	Dble	End	

Bacherich passed on the first round, hoping to draw the Brazilians into some later indiscretion. East passed also and South opened with a strong 2♣, overcalled by 2♠. Hoping to show how seriously he was taking this practice match for the world championship, Bacherich now bid 7♡.

At this stage you might think that East would give serious consideration to a sacrifice in spades. So he did, eventually deciding to pass. The French were about to enter the grand on their cards when they noticed that West was considering further action, despite his partner's hesitation. 'Seven Spades,' said West. '*Arbitre!*' cried the Frenchmen, proceeding to reserve their rights.

The auction continued. After two passes a piqued Deruy bid 7NT. This was doubled and went 2000 down on a spade lead. The Director ruled that West's spade sacrifice was in order, so the score stood. The Brazilians had bid and made 7♡ at the other table, so the total swing was 4210 – at that time worth 25 IMPs, the maximum possible. Shortly afterwards the IMP scale was redefined with the present maximum of 24 IMPs.

The Gambling 3NT opening, and the similar Gambling 3NT over-call, lead to many exciting situations. Sometimes the bid is doubled and large numbers of IMPs may hang on whether the declaring side stick to their guns or sound a retreat. A spectacular example of this situation occurred in the 1965 European Championship in Ostende.

The Italians had already qualified for the Bermuda Bowl, as holders, and had taken the opportunity to send some new faces to the European Championship. Belladonna, whose thirst for bridge was not easily quenched, joined the relatively unknown players.

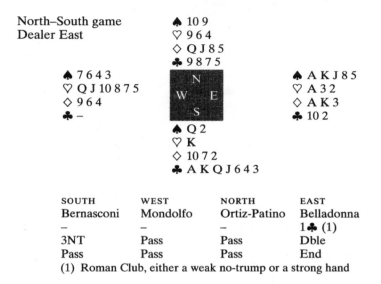

North–South game
Dealer East

	SOUTH	WEST	NORTH	EAST
	Bernasconi	Mondolfo	Ortiz-Patino	Belladonna
	–	–	–	1♣ (1)
	3NT	Pass	Pass	Dble
	Pass	Pass	Pass	End

(1) Roman Club, either a weak no-trump or a strong hand

Belladonna doubled 3NT and Bernasconi, who had described his hand, had no reason to run. Mondolfo did well to pass and all now depended on the action of Ortiz-Patino. With only 3 points, and just one suit stopped, the normal action is surely to remove to 4♣. Indeed, he should have made that bid on the previous round. No, he passed!

Renato Mondolfo, true to his Roman upbringing, led the jack of hearts. Belladonna put up the ace of hearts and declarer's king fell. The defenders soon had all 13 tricks pointing their way and that was a penalty of 2600, an all-time record in this event.

To the surprise of the kibitzers, there were no recriminations. When Ortiz-Patino was later asked how they had managed to retain their calm, he replied 'I am used to playing with Bernasconi. It happens to him all the time!' The question would have been better addressed to the other half of the partnership. Bernasconi's self-control was admirable.

The next deal features the biggest penalty ever seen in the Bermuda Bowl. Great Britain faced Sweden in a 1987 semi-final.

Game all
Dealer South

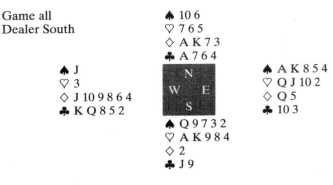

	♠ 10 6	
	♡ 7 6 5	
	◇ A K 7 3	
	♣ A 7 6 4	

♠ J   ♠ A K 8 5 4
♡ 3   ♡ Q J 10 2
◇ J 10 9 8 6 4   ◇ Q 5
♣ K Q 8 5 2   ♣ 10 3

       ♠ Q 9 7 3 2
       ♡ A K 9 8 4
       ◇ 2
       ♣ J 9

SOUTH	WEST	NORTH	EAST
Armstrong	Fallenius	Forrester	Lindkvist
2NT (1)	Pass	3♡ (2)	Pass
Pass	3NT	Dble	Pass
Pass	Rdble (3)	Pass	Pass
Pass	End		

(1) 7–10 points, a two-suiter not including clubs
(2) To be passed if partner has hearts, otherwise corrected
(3) SOS redouble: 'Please choose a minor suit'

Forrester responded 3♡ because he was willing to go as high as 4◇, should Armstrong hold spades and diamonds. This bid ran back to Fallenius. Unfortunately for him, a second interpretation of Forrester's 3♡ response was possible – that he held both majors and was happy to play in one of those, but not diamonds. In this case East–West might well have a good fit in one of the minors. Dangerous as it was, Fallenius decided to protect with an Unusual 3NT. The bid was not ambiguous because he had failed to say anything on the previous round.

Forrester doubled 3NT and Lindkvist passed. If this pass had the normal meaning, that East had no preference between his partner's suits, you would expect West to bid 4◇ now. No, Fallenius preferred an SOS redouble. He was horror-struck when the redouble was passed out. The British defenders showed no mercy, freezing the West hand out of action. The contract went five down redoubled for a penalty of 2800.

Why did East pass the redouble? He must have thought: 'A vulnerable partner would not come in on rubbish, just to protect a part-score. I have 12 points and both the majors stopped. Perhaps we can make this contract'. However, Forrester's double of 3NT made it unlikely that West held the 12 points or so which might give 3NT a chance. It was surely more likely that West had a shapely two-suiter in the minors and relatively few points. The result was a massive 21 IMPs to Great Britain and a devastating blow to the Swedes' morale. They never recovered and eventually lost the match by 47 IMPs.

We end the chapter in dramatic fashion, with perhaps the biggest penalty ever suffered in tournament play. Two teams packed with internationals met in the 1995 Spring Foursomes.

Game all
Dealer East

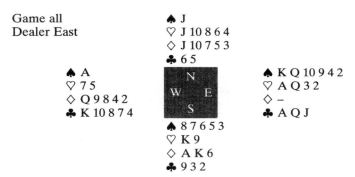

```
                    ♠ J
                    ♡ J 10 8 6 4
                    ◇ J 10 7 5 3
                    ♣ 6 5
  ♠ A                            ♠ K Q 10 9 4 2
  ♡ 7 5              N           ♡ A Q 3 2
  ◇ Q 9 8 4 2    W     E         ◇ –
  ♣ K 10 8 7 4      S            ♣ A Q J
                    ♠ 8 7 6 5 3
                    ♡ K 9
                    ◇ A K 6
                    ♣ 9 3 2
```

SOUTH	WEST	NORTH	EAST
Smolski	Shek	Sowter	Calderwood
–	–	–	1♣ (1)
1NT (2)	2◇ (3)	3♡ (4)	Dble
3♠ (5)	Pass	Pass	Dble
Pass	Pass	Rdble	End

(1) Strong Club, 17+ points
(2) Spades/diamonds, or hearts/clubs
(3) Natural response, 8+ points and at least 5 diamonds
(4) Assuming, after West's bid, that South has heart/clubs
(5) Showing spades/diamonds

Roman Smolski's 1NT overcall on a two-suiter that was only 5–3 is the sort of bid which is described as 'enterprising' when it succeeds, 'undisciplined' when it fails. His subsequent retreat to 3♠ indicated a two-suiter in spades and diamonds and one would therefore expect Tony Sowter to give preference to 4◇. He was dissuaded from this course by the fact that West had shown at least five diamonds himself! In case Smolski held some hand not matching his bidding, Sowter preferred an SOS redouble. Smolski should have removed the redouble, of course, but I can understand his reluctance to bid the three-card diamond suit when this had been called over him.

How many tricks would you expect declarer to make in 3♠

redoubled? He made none at all! Shek started brightly with the trump ace and switched to a diamond ruffed by his partner. Calderwood drew South's remaining trumps and the defenders continued mercilessly with five rounds of clubs. On the last round Smolski, down to $\heartsuit$ K 9 $\diamond$ A was caught in a defensive squeeze. He unguarded the heart king and East scored the last two tricks in hearts. Nine down for a penalty of 5200.

Team-mate, Keith Stanley, returned from the other table with a smile on his face. 'I think you're going to like this one,' he said, when the fateful board was reached. 'Plus 1460!'

'Ah, well done, you've saved an IMP,' replied Smolski. 'Just 23 away.'

4. Disaster at Both Tables

This chapter features deals where a top-class team suffered a disaster at both tables. As always we will survey the scene with an eagle-eye, trying to spot why things went wrong.

When Great Britain sat down to face USA in the 1965 Bermuda Bowl, a catastrophe of monumental proportions was about to strike them, the finger-signalling accusations against Reese and Schapiro. They had much the better of the match, in fact, despite a disaster at both tables on this deal:

North–South Game
Dealer South

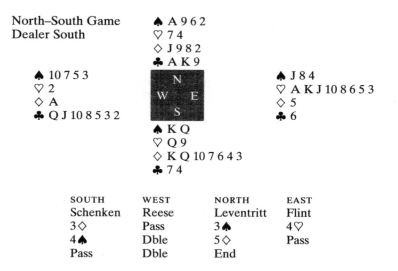

North:
♠ A 9 6 2
♡ 7 4
◇ J 9 8 2
♣ A K 9

West:
♠ 10 7 5 3
♡ 2
◇ A
♣ Q J 10 8 5 3 2

East:
♠ J 8 4
♡ A K J 10 8 6 5 3
◇ 5
♣ 6

South:
♠ K Q
♡ Q 9
◇ K Q 10 7 6 4 3
♣ 7 4

SOUTH	WEST	NORTH	EAST
Schenken	Reese	Leventritt	Flint
3◇	Pass	3♠	4♡
4♠	Dble	5◇	Pass
Pass	Dble	End	

Schenken's 3◇ opening was constructive and Leventritt responded 3♠ hoping partner held a heart stop and could bid 3NT. Flint entered with 4♡ and Schenken raised to the spade game, doubled by Reese. North retreated to 5◇, doubled again, and all now depended on the opening lead. What would you have led?

Since the opponents had bid game in spades, Reese expected Flint to hold at most one spade. He therefore led a spade. Schenken pitched a heart loser on the third round of spades and turned to the trump suit, soon claiming +750. Was Reese at fault with his lead? It seems so. If North held five spades he was unlikely to run from spades to diamonds, one level higher. And if North held only four spades, there was no

28

reason to place Flint with a singleton. Nor was it certain that Flint held a second trump, even if he had a spade singleton.

Even a club lead would have beaten the contract. Indeed, it would surely have led to a 500 penalty. Declarer would have won in dummy and unblocked his spade honours. When he attempted to cross to dummy with a club, to take a discard, East would ruff!

The British fared poorly at the other table too:

SOUTH	WEST	NORTH	EAST
Konstam	Petterson	Schapiro	Erdos
1◇	3♣	3NT	End

Schapiro's 3NT was eminently reasonable. Erdos was quick-witted enough to pass and it was the defenders who made 3NT rather than the declarer! That was 15 IMPs to USA, a minor prelude to the firework display that was about to erupt.

One of the game's worst *faux pas* is to double opponents into game. Can you believe that in a world championship final a team committed this offence at both tables on a single deal? It happened to the USA, facing the Italian Blue Team in the 1967 Bermuda Bowl.

Game all
Dealer West

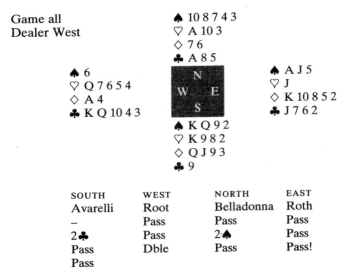

	♠ 10 8 7 4 3	
	♡ A 10 3	
	◇ 7 6	
	♣ A 8 5	

♠ 6   ♠ A J 5
♡ Q 7 6 5 4   ♡ J
◇ A 4   ◇ K 10 8 5 2
♣ K Q 10 4 3   ♣ J 7 6 2

♠ K Q 9 2
♡ K 9 8 2
◇ Q J 9 3
♣ 9

SOUTH	WEST	NORTH	EAST
Avarelli	Root	Belladonna	Roth
–	Pass	Pass	Pass
2♣	Pass	2♠	Pass
Pass	Dble	Pass	Pass!
Pass			

How many players today would pass on those West cards? Avarelli opened in the fourth seat with a Roman 2♣. This showed 12–16 points and an unspecified three-suiter. Belladonna's 2♠ was to be passed unless this happened to be South's singleton (it is rather a surprising response since the auction might then be carried to the three-level).

When the bidding reverted to William Root he reasoned: the opponents have found a spade fit and stopped low; we should have around half the points and a fit somewhere ourselves. This was correctly judged. Since he would have re-opened with 2NT if he held both minors, his actual double suggested hearts and another (or a three-suiter outside spades). Had East–West landed in 3♣, all would have been well. No, instead of responding 3♣ (or, better, 2NT to show both minors) Roth passed the double out! Belladonna made his contract with an overtrick and the Italians picked up +870.

This was the bidding at the other table:

SOUTH	WEST	NORTH	EAST
Kehela	Forquet	Murray	Garozzo
–	Pass	Pass	Pass
1◇	1♡	1♠	Pass
Pass	2♣	2♠	3♣
3♠	4♣	Dble	End

It seems that a trump lead might have beaten the contract, but South comes under too much pressure and declarer can always succeed. In fact a diamond was led and, after various twists and turns, Forquet emerged with ten tricks and +710. The Italians had gained 17 IMPs on a part-score deal!

What do you make of the Canadians' bidding? Kehela should surely have raised to 2♠, rather than hope to buy it at the one-level. Murray's final double seems too close for comfort. He had no surprise for the opponents. Nor, being vulnerable, were they likely to have bid more than one trick beyond their playing strength.

The Americans fared poorly in the 1969 Bermuda Bowl, triggering a famous sequence of articles by Kaplan in *Bridge World*. 'Disaster in Rio', was the title he chose. Somewhat against the flow, it was the Italians who had a double disaster on this deal:

North–South game
Dealer West

♠ 6 5
♡ Q 7 6
♦ A Q 10 6 2
♣ A 6 5

♠ Q 4
♡ K 8 5 4 3 2
♦ 9 8
♣ K 8 4

N
W E
S

♠ K J 9 8 3 2
♡ J 10
♦ J 7 3
♣ 10 2

♠ A 10 7
♡ A 9
♦ K 5 4
♣ Q J 9 7 3

SOUTH	WEST	NORTH	EAST
Belladonna	Kantar	Avarelli	Hamman
–	Pass	1♣ (1)	1♠
2♠ (2)	Pass	3♦	Pass
3NT	End		

(1) Roman Club, 12–16 balanced or various strong types
(2) Asking for a spade stop

Belladonna arrived in 3NT and West led ♠Q. The diamond suit will come in and the club finesse is onside. Can you imagine how the Italian maestro went down?

Belladonna placed the heart and club kings with East and sought to make his contract via an endplay. He won the very first spade (to allow him to later exit in spades from the dummy), then ran the diamond suit. Hamman discarded ♣2 followed by ♡10, retaining five spade winners. With some confidence, Belladonna played a heart to the ace, then a club to the ace. Neither king fell and the contract was one down! West held both missing kings, despite East's overcall.

This was the bidding at the other table:

SOUTH	WEST	NORTH	EAST
Lazard	Garozzo	Rapée	Forquet
–	Pass	1♦	1♠
2♣	2♡	3♣	Pass
3♠	Dble	Pass	Pass
6♣	End		

That final bid looks bold to me, but all turned out well. Sidney Lazard won the spade lead and ran the trump queen successfully, drawing the 4 and the 2. Suppose you had been the declarer. How would you have continued the trump suit?

According to contemporary reports, Lazard reasoned that if East held ♣10 8 2 he might well have false-carded the 8 on the first round, hoping to induce a misguess. If East held ♣10 2, he would be forced to play the 2. Lazard led the jack on the second round and duly made the slam. 18 IMPs to USA.

The 'lack of false-card' argument is debatable. A better reason for playing as declarer did is this: West is more likely to cover the queen when he holds king doubleton. Suppose he didn't cover from king doubleton and the trump suit lay like this:

♣ A 6 5

♣ K 4   ♣ 10 9 2

♣ Q J 8 7 3

Declarer would pick up the suit without loss!

Jeff Rubens and Edgar Kaplan were co-authors of the venerable *Bridge World* magazine for more than three decades. In the trials to decide the second USA team for the 1973 Bermuda Bowl they found themselves in opposition. Jeff's team won by a fair margin despite a double disaster on this deal:

North–South game	♠ J 8 6 5 3 2	
Dealer West	♡ 10	
	◇ 10 7 3	
	♣ 10 5 3	

♠ Q 10 7 4   ♠ A K 9

♡ J 8 7 6   ♡ K 4 3

◇ Q 9 8 6 4   ◇ K J 5 2

♣ –   ♣ A K 6

♠ –

♡ A Q 9 5 2

◇ A

♣ Q J 9 8 7 4 2

SOUTH	WEST	NORTH	EAST
Grieve	Bernstein	Rapée	Becker
–	Pass	Pass	2NT
3♣ (1)	Pass	4♠	Pass
5♣	Pass	Pass	Dble
End			

(1) Landy, promising length in both majors!

Billy Grieve, an IBM systems programmer (like myself) was in two minds over B. J. Becker's 2NT opening. He wanted to say something but 3♣ would be conventional, showing the majors. He decided to risk the bid anyway, intending to correct the likely 3♠ response to 4♣. Unfortunately his partner held six spades and bumped the bidding all the way to 4♠. Grieve now had to correct to 5♣, which Becker was pleased to double on the way out.

A trump lead would have put the contract two down. West was on lead, however, with no route to his partner's hand. The contract could not be defeated and Grieve scored +750. At the other table John Swanson (South) passed over 2NT and failed to compete when East–West bid to 3NT. This was over-cautious. South's clubs were fairly solid and 4♣ was unlikely to go for a big number. That was another 430 to Kaplan's team, a swing of 15 IMPs.

The Italian ladies claimed the gold medals at the 1976 Olympiad but not before they had suffered a double disaster on this board, played against the British.

```
Game all              ♠ Q 6 4 2
Dealer South          ♡ J 7 5
                      ◇ 9 8 6 3
                      ♣ 8 6
        ♠ K                            ♠ J 10 7
        ♡ A 8 6 3          N          ♡ K Q 10 4 2
        ◇ A J 5 4       W     E       ◇ K Q 10 2
        ♣ Q J 7 5          S          ♣ 2
                      ♠ A 9 8 5 3
                      ♡ 9
                      ◇ 7
                      ♣ A K 10 9 4 3
```

SOUTH	WEST	NORTH	EAST
Oldroyd	Bianchi	Esterson	Valenti
1♣	Pass	Pass	Dble
Pass	Pass	Rdble	End

Bianchi decided to leave in her partner's take-out double of 1♣. The British North, Charlie Esterson, then made an SOS redouble to request a rescue. Rita Oldroyd could have run to spades but the opponents would then doubtless have bid their cold heart game. She judged well to stay exactly where she was – in 1♣ redoubled.

Bianchi saw little reason to fear the situation. Did she not hold 15 points, facing a take-out double from partner, and Q J x x in trumps sitting over declarer? Oldroyd had no difficulty in making an overtrick, however, and that was +580 to North–South. (With the improved redoubled 'insult' bonus, it would nowadays be +630.)

Look back to Bianchi's pass of 1♣ doubled. How did it strike you? Many players pass on such hands, reckoning it to be the standard action. Look at it this way, though. For South's contract to go one down, you will need to make seven tricks in a probable 4–1 trump fit. If this feat proves to be achievable, would it not have been easier to make nine tricks in no-trumps? Also, a no-trump game is worth 600 rather than 200. West should surely have bid 3NT rather than pass the double of 1♣.

This was the bidding at the other table:

SOUTH	WEST	NORTH	EAST
Capodanno	Gardener	d'Andrea	Landy
1♠	Dble	2♠	4♡
4♠	Dble	End	

Nothing much wrong with the bidding but the Italian declarer misjudged the play. Nicola Gardener led ace and another heart, forcing the South hand. Had Capodanno laid down the trump ace now, she would have made the contract (by cashing one high club, crossing to the trump queen, and leading a second club towards the king).

The Italian declarer preferred to lead a low trump towards dummy. West won with the bare trump king and played another heart, shortening South once more. Capodanno cashed the ace of clubs, played a trump to the queen, and led a club towards her hand. Sandra Landy refused to ruff and declarer won with the club king. A club was ruffed in dummy and overruffed. The defenders resumed their force on the South hand and the Italians lost 800 instead of gaining 790. 16 IMPs away.

You would like to see the ultimate 'disaster at both tables' scenario? How about a situation where a side concedes a slam at each table, and both the slams could have been beaten in top cards? It happened when Canada faced South Africa during the 1995 Bermuda Bowl in Beijing.

Game all
Dealer West

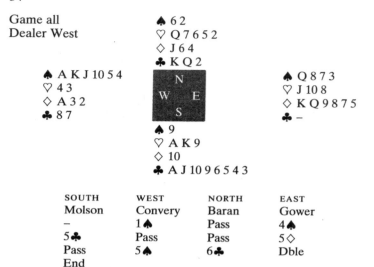

```
                      ♠ 6 2
                      ♡ Q 7 6 5 2
                      ◇ J 6 4
                      ♣ K Q 2
   ♠ A K J 10 5 4                      ♠ Q 8 7 3
   ♡ 4 3              N                ♡ J 10 8
   ◇ A 3 2        W       E            ◇ K Q 9 8 7 5
   ♣ 8 7              S                ♣ —
                      ♠ 9
                      ♡ A K 9
                      ◇ 10
                      ♣ A J 10 9 6 5 4 3
```

SOUTH	WEST	NORTH	EAST
Molson	Convery	Baran	Gower
–	1♠	Pass	4♠
5♣	Pass	Pass	5◇
Pass	5♠	6♣	Dble
End			

The Canadians arrived in Six Clubs doubled and Convery led ◇ A, East playing the 9. What next? Fearing that declarer was void in spades, West continued with a second diamond. Curtains! Declarer ruffed, drew trumps, and discarded his spade loser on dummy's heart suit.

Could this disaster have been avoided, do you think? The normal signalling method for cashing out against high contracts is to lead 'king for count' and 'ace for attitude'. (You lead the king from ace-king to discover whether a second round will stand up.) Here the situation was somewhat different. East had made a lead-directing bid in diamonds and would surely hold the king of that suit. On that basis East's ◇9 should be interpreted as a count signal. Not a certain guide here, as it happens, because East might hold a 5–3–4–1 or 5–4–4–0 hand.

This was the auction at the other table:

SOUTH	WEST	NORTH	EAST
Mansell	Silver	Cope	Kokish
–	1♠	Pass	2◇
3♣	3♠	5♣	5♠
6♣	Pass	Pass	6♠
End			

North led ♣K and an easy overtrick resulted. The Canadians added 1460 to the 1540 from the other table, giving them a swing of 22 IMPs.

I can see no reason to fault North for his lead. Could South have helped in any way? Holding eight clubs, he could be almost certain that a club lead was no good. Unfortunately for him, a Lightner Double would surely attract a diamond lead rather than a heart. One, slightly obscure, possibility remains. Perhaps South could have bid 5NT instead of 6♣! Since a Lightner Double was available to request a diamond lead, this manoeuvre (which could only be lead-directing) would suggest the lead of a heart. Something to think about.

On now to a hand that must surely hold a world record of some sort. Ukraine faced France in the 1996 Olympiad in Rhodes.

North–South game
Dealer South

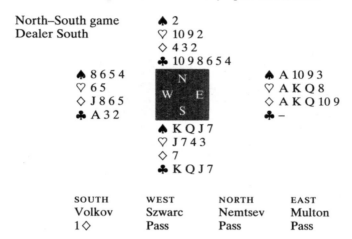

	♠ 2	
	♡ 10 9 2	
	◇ 4 3 2	
	♣ 10 9 8 6 5 4	

♠ 8 6 5 4		♠ A 10 9 3
♡ 6 5		♡ A K Q 8
◇ J 8 6 5		◇ A K Q 10 9
♣ A 3 2		♣ –

	♠ K Q J 7
	♡ J 7 4 3
	◇ 7
	♣ K Q J 7

SOUTH	WEST	NORTH	EAST
Volkov	Szwarc	Nemtsev	Multon
1◇	Pass	Pass	Pass

The Ukrainians were playing a strong club system, with 5-card majors. Not the best of methods when you pick up that South hand! Volkov was forced to open 1◇ and Multon judged well to pass on the East cards. Declarer scored just two spade tricks in his bizarre contract, conceding a penalty of 500.

Ending in a 3–1 fit is a considerable feat but on the very same deal Volkov's team-mates managed to outshine him! This was the auction at the other table, with the Ukrainians sitting East–West:

SOUTH	WEST	NORTH	EAST
Lévy	Mikhaylenko	Mouiel	Livshitis
1♣	Pass	Pass	2♣
Pass	Pass!	Pass	End

East intended his 2♣ to show a game-going hand but his partner read the bid as natural. This interpretation made little sense. If East held long clubs he would surely pass out 1♣, letting the vulnerable opponents struggle there. The 2♣ contract went two down and that was 12 IMPs to the French. The Ukrainians had played in a 3–1 fit at one table, a 3–0 fit at the other.

The Ukrainian team clearly saw no reason to change their methods after this disaster. A year later, facing the Italians in the 1997 European Championships, Gladyh of Ukraine held this hand:

> ♠ J 7 6
> ♡ A Q 6 4
> ◇ K 3
> ♣ J 10 8 6

Vulnerable against not, in the third seat, he opened 1◇! Versace, next to speak, held a balanced 17-count including ◇A J 9 8 6. He found a smart pass and was rewarded when, after a pass by the second Ukrainian, his partner re-opened with a double. There was no further bidding and Gladyh scored just one trick, with the heart ace. The Italians picked up 1700, gaining 16 IMPs against the no-trump game made at the other table. What could be *gained* by opening 1◇ on such a hand? That's the question I would ask.

USA I and USA II, arch-rival teams, met in the semi-finals of the 1997 Bermuda Bowl. The biggest swing of the whole tournament arose on this deal:

East–West game	♠ 9 8 7 4		
Dealer North	♡ 4		
	◇ 6		
	♣ A K Q 9 5 3 2		

♠ 5 2		♠ A Q 3
♡ –		♡ K Q 10 7 3 2
◇ A J 10 8 7 4 2		◇ K 9 5 3
♣ J 10 6 4		♣ –

> ♠ K J 10 6
> ♡ A J 9 8 6 5
> ◇ Q
> ♣ 8 7

SOUTH	WEST	NORTH	EAST
Rodwell	Martel	Meckstroth	Stansby
–	–	3♠ (1)	4♡
Dble	End		

(1) Unspecified solid suit

Stansby played well to escape for 800 but, as you see, the East–West hands belong in diamonds. Indeed, a small slam in diamonds would have been straightforward. Was either player to blame, do you think?

Let's consider first whether West should have rescued into Five Diamonds. Some players are rescuers by nature. 'It's not going to be a good board in Four Hearts doubled,' they say. 'There's nothing much to lose by trying Five Diamonds.' Well, they would have been right on this hand.

I am not a rescuer myself and would have matched Martel's pass on the West cards. I am more inclined to look closely at East's 4♡ overcall. On a hand that could play in three denominations, it would perhaps have been better to start with a double (showing points rather than spades). If this is followed by two passes and the expected retreat by North to 4♣, you can bid 4♡ then, having told partner that your hand is playable elsewhere. It's not just a matter of finding the correct trump suit, you are more likely to detect a playable slam this way.

At the other table North found a less challenging opening bid.

SOUTH	WEST	NORTH	EAST
Soloway	Freeman	Deutsch	Nickell
–	–	1♣	1♡
Pass	2♦	3♣	4♣
4♠	5♦	Pass	6♦
Dble	End		

It was a great effort to reach the diamond slam and Freeman added 1540 to the 800 from the other table, a swing of 20 IMPs.

A decisive feature on the deal was the choice of opening bid on the North hand. Should a holding of four small in a major deter you from a pre-emptive opening? The text books may say so. Look through any world championship book, however, and you will see that the top players turn a blind eye to such advice.

At IMP-scoring it is sometimes held to be lucky when your team encounters two poor results on the same board. 'Look on the bright side,' says a team-mate, whose absurd overcall has just gone for 1100. 'The disasters would have cost much more if they'd happened on separate boards.'

True enough. But you can't afford too many lucky breaks of this sort.

5. Blackwood Disasters

It seems a simple convention, Blackwood, but there are several ways in which it can go wrong. If you over-estimate the playing strength of the two hands, for example, the Blackwood response may carry you past the safe level. That's what happened to the Australian women when they faced Egypt in the 1987 Venice Cup.

Love all
Dealer North

	♠ 10 5	
	♡ Q J 10 4	
	♢ 2	
	♣ A K Q 8 7 3	

♠ A J		♠ 9 8 7 6 4 3
♡ A 6 5 3	N	♡ 7
♢ A 10 9 7	W E	♢ 8 6 5 4 3
♣ 5 4 2	S	♣ 6

	♠ K Q 2	
	♡ K 9 8 2	
	♢ K Q J	
	♣ J 10 9	

SOUTH	WEST	NORTH	EAST
Lester	Sidhorn	Courtney	Morcos
–	–	1♣	Pass
1♡	Pass	4♢ (1)	Pass
4NT (2)	Pass	5♢ (3)	Pass
5♠ (4)	Pass	6♣ (5)	Pass
6♡	Dble	End	

(1) Splinter bid, a raise to 4♡ with at most one diamond
(2) Roman Key-Card Blackwood
(3) 1 or 4 'key cards' (the four aces and the trump king)
(4) Have you the queen of trumps?   (5) Yes, and club king

The Australian South assumed four key cards, rather than one, and proceeded to ask for the trump queen. There was little point to this further inquiry since North would hardly have opened only 1♣ if she held the 23 points needed for a grand slam (♠A ♡A Q ♢A ♣A K Q). The Egyptian West doubled 6♡ and was pleased to find all three of her aces standing up.

What do you make of the auction? All Blackwood users should follow this sound rule: whenever it is possible that partner has 1 key card rather than 4 (or 0 rather than 3), the 4NT bidder should sign off. Partner will then advance with the more generous allocation. Here South should have bid 5 ♡ over 5 ♢, knowing that partner would bid on with four key-cards. It would not have saved many points on this particular deal, but it is a good practice to acquire.

With ten tricks the limit, we must next ask whether either North or South overbid. North was sub-minimum for her splinter bid and most players would have rebid only 3 ♡ on her hand. In general, there is no need to overbid on shapely hands with relatively few points. Particularly when the opponents are silent, partner will usually have enough spare points to pull in the slack. South overstated her values too. Fifteen points, yes, but the six points in diamonds were unlikely to pull much weight, facing a shortage.

We'll look now at another possible source of confusion: Does partner intend 4NT as Roman Key-Card Blackwood (with a trump suit agreed), or as straight four-ace Blackwood? For example, suppose partner opens 1 ♠ and you hold this freak hand:

♠ 5
♡ A K Q J
♢ K Q J 10 9 7 3
♣ A

You bid 4NT and he responds 5 ♡. With two aces opposite, you may think that 7NT will stand a chance. Not if partner has interpreted 4NT as Roman Key-Card for spades and his two key-cards are the spade ace and king!

Some partnerships say that 4NT is RKCB if a suit has been agreed, normal Blackwood otherwise. But there are always borderline cases where one player assumes a trump suit has been agreed, his partner does not. Two of the game's most famous names encountered this problem in the 1981 NatWest Trophy, contested in Manchester. This was the deal:

Game all   ♠ 4 3
Dealer West   ♡ K J 10 8 3 2
             ♢ K Q J 3
             ♣ 5

♠ J 8 7 2
♡ 9
♢ 10 8 5 4
♣ 10 9 8 3

♠ –
♡ A Q 7
♢ 9 7 6 2
♣ K Q J 7 6 2

♠ A K Q 10 9 6 5
♡ 6 5 4
♢ A
♣ A 4

SOUTH	WEST	NORTH	EAST
Sharif		Chemla	
–	Pass	1♡	3♣
4NT	5♣	Pass	Pass
7♠	Pass	Pass	Dble
7NT	Pass	Pass	Dble
End			

Sharif and Chemla were employing the DOPI convention over Blackwood interference. (The DOPI acronym stands for Double: 0, Pass: 1.) Chemla had interpreted the 4NT bid as Roman Key-Card Blackwood and intended his pass over 5♣ to indicate one key-card, the king of trumps.

Omar Sharif, however, thought that no suit had been agreed and that his 4NT had asked only for aces. Assuming from partner's pass over 5♣ that he held the ace of hearts, Sharif ventured a grand slam in spades. East now made a Lightner Double, for a heart lead. Thinking that East might be void in hearts, Sharif corrected the contract to 7NT. East doubled again and won the heart lead with the queen. With the contract already beaten, he played ♣K, rather than cash a second heart. Sharif ended with only five tricks and East–West collected a famous 2300!

A disaster of a different sort happened to Sweden's Lindkvist and Sundelin on the same board. GCH Fox, South, arrived in Six Spades. Sundelin doubled for a heart lead (North having opened 1♡) but Lindkvist led a club. Foxy won with the ace, drew one round of trumps, and unblocked ♢A. He entered dummy with a club ruff and threw all three hearts on dummy's top diamonds. He had to lose a trump trick but it was still +1660 to North–South.

How rare do you think it is, in a major championship, for a grand

slam to be bid with the ace of trumps missing? In the 1991 European
Championships seven teams achieved that feat!

Game all   ♠ K Q J 9 2
Dealer North   ♡ K Q
                ◇ K Q 8 7 6
                ♣ 10

♠ 8 6 4 3			♠ 10 7 5
♡ J 9 7 6 5 2	N		♡ 10 8 4
◇ –	W E		◇ A
♣ J 5 3	S		♣ K 9 8 6 4 2

                ♠ A
                ♡ A 3
                ◇ J 10 9 5 4 3 2
                ♣ A Q 7

SOUTH	WEST	NORTH	EAST
Sowter	Chnaris	Smolski	Giannoutsos
–	–	1♠	Pass
2◇	Pass	4◇	Pass
4NT	Pass	5◇	Pass
6♣	Pass	7◇	Dble
End			

Facing jump-support, Tony Sowter could expect no losers outside
the trump suit. Roman Key-Card Blackwood discovered only one key-
card opposite. If this was the trump ace, there would be some play for
the grand. Indeed, it would be cold if partner had ◇A Q 8 7 6; the
outstanding king would be singleton. Seeking assistance on the matter,
Sowter made a grand slam try of 6♣. Smolski could hardly visualise
that the trump ace was missing. He had announced only one key-card
and partner was still interested in a grand slam. Since his own hand was
solid, bar the four aces, he was surely entitled to bid 7◇.
    The result was duplicated at the other table:

SOUTH	WEST	NORTH	EAST
Lambrinos	Robson	Kannavos	Forrester
–	–	1♠	Pass
2◇	Pass	4NT	Pass
5♣	Pass	6◇	Pass
7◇	Pass	Pass	Dble
End			

North could not be certain of three aces opposite, merely because his partner had responded at the two level. His Blackwood call was an overbid and would have carried his side too high, had South held only two aces.

South must take a fair share of the blame too. The raise to 7♢ was undisciplined. His partner had made no attempt to investigate a grand slam after the three-ace response. The possession of two extra trumps and the club queen was scarcely sufficient to overrule partner's decision.

Amazingly, this grand slam missing the ace of trumps was bid also by Bulgaria, Czechoslovakia, Germany, Ireland and Liechtenstein. Poland attempted to outshine them by bidding 7NT. I am reminded of a famous quip from Boris Schapiro. 'Priday and Rodrigue bid an excellent grand slam but the ace of trumps was offside. Such bad luck, it could happen to anyone!'

Now for the most notorious Blackwood Disaster of all time – a grand slam with four aces missing. It happened during the final qualifying round of the 1971 Bermuda Bowl. This was the deal:

Love all
Dealer South

```
                    ♠ K J 4 3
                    ♡ 10 9 7 2
                    ◇ J 9 7 6 2
                    ♣ –
    ♠ 8 6 2              N              ♠ A 10 9 7 5
    ♡ A 5 4         W         E         ♡ 6
    ◇ A 10 5            S              ◇ K 8 4 3
    ♣ A 5 4 2                          ♣ 8 7 6
                    ♠ Q
                    ♡ K Q J 8 3
                    ◇ Q
                    ♣ K Q J 10 9 3
```

SOUTH	WEST	NORTH	EAST
Trézel	D'Ave	Stoppa	Chagas
1♣	Pass	1◇	Pass
1♡	Pass	3♡	Pass
4NT	Pass	5♣ (1)	Pass
7♡	Dble	End	

(1) 0 or 4 aces

The French team had already qualified for the next stage and, at the captain's suggestion, had switched into unfamiliar partnerships. Stoppa intended his 3♡ as a limit bid. Trézel read it as forcing and proceeded with Blackwood. In those days the 5♣ response showed 0 or 4 aces. Since North could hardly have made a forcing raise on two kings and two jacks, Trézel assumed four aces opposite and bid the grand. The Brazilian West ventured a double and the grand went three down.

I'll end the chapter with a small Blackwood adventure that I encountered myself. Playing in the 1988 Pachabo Cup (English inter-county Teams of Four championship), vulnerable against not, I picked up this hand:

♠ A
♡ J 9 4
♢ 3
♣ K Q J 10 9 7 5 2

John Elliot opened a multi 2◇ on my right, indicating a weak two in one of the majors or various strong hands. I leapt to 4♣ and Sandra Landy, on my left, contested with a natural 4◇. Richard Hyde, my partner, completed an eventful first round of bidding with 4NT (normal Blackwood).

Looking at the hand now, in the cold light of day, I see no reason to be ashamed of it. Back in 1988 I feared I was somewhat light for my previous bid and decided to hide an ace. This would also keep us at a safe level if Richard, a notorious overbidder, had risked Blackwood when holding only one ace. I responded 5♣, denying any aces, and Richard promptly bid 7♣.

Aagh! The 5♣ response had shown 0 or 3 aces and he was placing me with three. I was ready to take my medicine but, wait a moment, John Elliot was still thinking.

'What was the 4NT?' enquired Elliot.

'Normal Blackwood,' I replied coolly.

'And the Five Club response?' he continued.

'Nought or three aces,' replied Richard Hyde.

Elliot paused for a few more seconds. 'Seven Diamonds,' he said.

Reprieved from the noose, I doubled. Thunder was gathering on my left. 'Pass me my cigarettes, John!' exclaimed Sandra Landy.

This was the full deal:

East–West game
Dealer North

♠ Q 10 8 7 6 2
♡ 8 3 2
♢ K 9 5 4
♣ —

♠ J 3
♡ K Q 10 7 5
♢ Q 7
♣ A 8 4 3

♠ A
♡ J 9 4
♢ 3
♣ K Q J 10 9 7 5 2

♠ K 9 5 4
♡ A 6
♢ A J 10 8 6 2
♣ 6

SOUTH	WEST	NORTH	EAST
Landy	Hyde	Elliot	Bird
–	–	2♢ (1)	4♣
4♢	4NT	Pass	5♣
Pass	7♣	7♢	Dble
End			

(1) Multi, usually a weak two in a major

Richard led ♡K and Sandra Landy won pointedly with the ace.
'Sorry, partner,' mumbled poor John Elliot.
'There's another ace to come!' barked Landy.

So, there's no real need to fear Blackwood disasters. You can still
end with a good board, even when you're playing against a world
champion. Does anything else occur to you on this deal? It's taken me
over a decade to notice that the opening lead was out of turn!

6. Disastrous Defences

Defence is a difficult art and without a sight of partner's hand it is not possible to find the right play all the time. In this chapter we will look at some deals where the world's top players have – not to put too fine a point on it – screwed up in defence. Our task, as always, will be to see how they might have done better.

We travel back into the mists of time for our first deal, to the famous match played between Culbertson and Beasley in 1933.

East–West game
Dealer South

	♠ A	
	♡ J 8 6 5	
	◇ A K 10 7 5 3 2	
	♣ 5	

♠ K 5		♠ J 10 8 7 6 4
♡ K 10	N	♡ Q 3 2
◇ Q J 6 4	W E	◇ 8
♣ A K J 7 4	S	♣ 8 6 2

	♠ Q 9 3 2	
	♡ A 9 7 4	
	◇ 9	
	♣ Q 10 9 3	

SOUTH	WEST	NORTH	EAST
Domville	Culbertson	Beasley	Lightner
Pass	1♣	2◇	Pass
2NT	Pass	3NT	Pass
Pass	Dble	4◇	Pass
4NT	Dble	End	

The bidding was unimpressive. Colonel Beasley had no reason to pull 3NT doubled, with his fine diamond suit and an outside ace. When the double was pulled South should expect his partner's diamonds to be long but broken, not at all what would be needed for 4NT to be a success. However . . .

Domville won the ♣7 lead with the 10. When he led ◇9, Culbertson covered! This ensured six diamond tricks for declarer, who might well have intended to rise with dummy's ace, to keep East off lead. Domville won with the ace and continued with the king and 10 of diamonds, clearing the suit. Meanwhile Lightner threw ♠6 followed by ♠4, the high–low suggesting that he held something good in the suit. Culbertson cashed ♣K, to alert partner to the situation there, then switched to ♠5.

Declarer won with the spade ace and ran the diamond suit, keeping ♠Q ♡A ♣Q. Culbertson had to find one more discard from ♠K ♡K 10 ♣A. Since Lightner had echoed in spades, and declarer might well hold ♡A Q, he chose to throw ♠K. Sir Guy Domville now scored ♡A and ♠Q for the contract!

Culbertson blamed his mis-reading of the end position on partner's earlier echo in spades. But if South's last three cards were ♡A Q ♣Q, as Culbertson thought, East would have started with ♠Q J 10 8 7 6 4. He would surely have thrown the spade queen at some stage, to clarify the position in that suit.

Some three decades later, in the 1961 Bermuda Bowl, we can expect the standard of defence to have improved. Let's see.

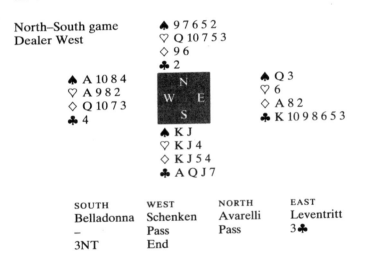

North–South game	♠ 9 7 6 5 2
Dealer West	♡ Q 10 7 5 3
	◇ 9 6
	♣ 2

♠ A 10 8 4		♠ Q 3
♡ A 9 8 2		♡ 6
◇ Q 10 7 3		◇ A 8 2
♣ 4		♣ K 10 9 8 6 5 3

	♠ K J
	♡ K J 4
	◇ K J 5 4
	♣ A Q J 7

SOUTH	WEST	NORTH	EAST
Belladonna	Schenken	Avarelli	Leventritt
–	Pass	Pass	3♣
3NT	End		

Schenken led his singleton club and Leventritt contributed the king, giving declarer three club tricks. Do you think it was right to play the king? It would gain only when partner had led from ♣Q 7 4. This would leave declarer with only ♣A J, when a take-out double would usually be more attractive than 3NT.

The no-trump game still seemed a hopeless proposition. At trick two Belladonna led the king of spades, which was allowed to hold. Schenken placed declarer with the spade queen and hoped that his subsequent continuation would become clearer if he delayed taking the top spade. Off to a good start, Belladonna now turned to hearts.

The king won the first round and the jack, also ducked, was overtaken with dummy's queen. Now came a diamond to the jack and queen.

Schenken cashed the heart ace, a sensible move that might prevent a later end-play. He continued with the spade ace, dropping the queen and jack. This position had been reached:

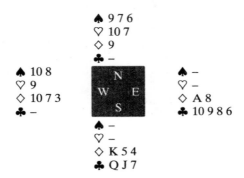

Schenken, one of bridge's all-time great players, now inexplicably played a heart. Belladonna scored dummy's two winners in the suit, throwing a diamond and a club, then led towards the diamond king. Nine tricks!

In the diagrammed position West should have cashed his master spade, then exited with ◇10. This would beat the contract unless South held an impregnable ◇A K 8 ♣Q J 7.

You may think that this was just careless play, with no lesson for us to draw. I believe there is one. When things have gone badly wrong, either in defending or playing the dummy, do not drop your guard. Stop for a while to re-assess the situation. Perhaps all is not lost. Give the same amount of effort to the remaining tricks as you would do normally.

I might have included this deal in the 'Disaster at both Tables' chapter. When it was replayed, Garozzo (the Italian East) passed and Silodor opened 1♣ on the South cards. Forquet doubled and, when three passes ensued, made the book lead of a trump. Silodor scored only three trump tricks and the diamond king, going 800 down for an 18-IMP loss.

France faced USA in the final of the 1982 Rosenblum Cup. The French defenders were playing competent signalling methods, as you would expect, but still went astray on this hand:

Love all
Dealer South

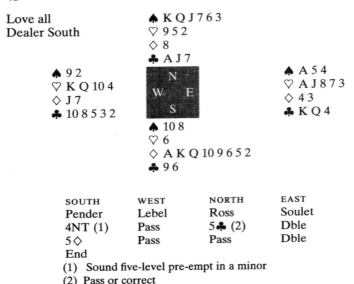

	♠ K Q J 7 6 3	
	♡ 9 5 2	
	◇ 8	
	♣ A J 7	
♠ 9 2		♠ A 5 4
♡ K Q 10 4		♡ A J 8 7 3
◇ J 7		◇ 4 3
♣ 10 8 5 3 2		♣ K Q 4
	♠ 10 8	
	♡ 6	
	◇ A K Q 10 9 6 5 2	
	♣ 9 6	

SOUTH	WEST	NORTH	EAST
Pender	Lebel	Ross	Soulet
4NT (1)	Pass	5♣ (2)	Dble
5◇	Pass	Pass	Dble
End			

(1) Sound five-level pre-empt in a minor
(2) Pass or correct

The contract was the same at both tables and the two West players led ♡K. What type of signal would you expect East to give? Most experts nowadays follow the scheme of giving count on a king lead, attitude on the lead of an ace or queen. The French stars were using this method and Soulet duly signalled with the 3, showing three or five hearts. What should Lebel do next?

A club switch is attractive (it beat the contract at the other table, where the bidding had been a simpler 5◇ – Pass – Pass – Dble). Here, however, East had also doubled 5♣ and might be thought to hold something good in the suit. Lebel was worried that declarer was void in clubs. A club switch would then allow him to discard a heart (from a 3-card holding). Nor would a club switch gain when East held four clubs. It was only when East held three or fewer clubs that a club switch could be necessary.

After this pre-amble you can guess what happened. Lebel talked himself out of a club switch and played another heart. Pender ruffed, drew trumps, and set up the spades to discard his club loser. +550 and a swing of 12 IMPs.

How much blame should be attributed to Lebel? It was certainly possible that declarer was void in clubs but if his hand were such as ♠10 8 ♡J 8 6 ◇A K Q 10 9 6 5 2 ♣– the contract would at least still go one down on a club switch. West's actual heart continuation was much more dangerous, it risked conceding the contract.

Does anything else strike you? Philippe Soulet, the French East, was not blameless! He could have ensured defeat of the contract by overtaking the king of hearts with the ace and switching to the king of clubs.

If your life depended on some player successfully defending a no-play grand slam, who would you choose to represent you? Paul Chemla, perhaps? Sorry, you may not have made a wise choice. This deal arose in the 1991 Cap Gemini tournament.

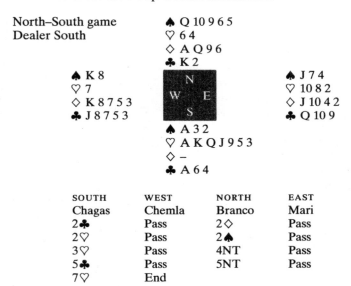

North–South game
Dealer South

♠ Q 10 9 6 5
♡ 6 4
◊ A Q 9 6
♣ K 2

♠ K 8
♡ 7
◊ K 8 7 5 3
♣ J 8 7 5 3

♠ J 7 4
♡ 10 8 2
◊ J 10 4 2
♣ Q 10 9

♠ A 3 2
♡ A K Q J 9 5 3
◊ —
♣ A 6 4

SOUTH	WEST	NORTH	EAST
Chagas	Chemla	Branco	Mari
2♣	Pass	2◊	Pass
2♡	Pass	2♠	Pass
3♡	Pass	4NT	Pass
5♣	Pass	5NT	Pass
7♡	End		

The Brazilians were playing normal Blackwood. 5NT confirmed that all aces were present, thereby inviting a grand slam. In the absence of Roman Key-Card Blackwood, Gabriel Chagas had not yet had an opportunity to show that his trumps were solid. Eventually he concluded that his fine trumps entitled him to bid the grand.

A club was led and Chagas took the king and ace, ruffing the third round. He then ran the trump suit, arriving at this end position:

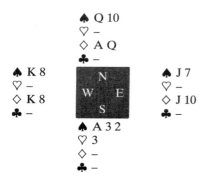

```
              ♠ Q 10
              ♡ –
              ◇ A Q
              ♣ –
♠ K 8                        ♠ J 7
♡ –          N              ♡ –
◇ K 8      W   E            ◇ J 10
♣ –          S              ♣ –
              ♠ A 3 2
              ♡ 3
              ◇ –
              ♣ –
```

When the last trump was led Chemla threw ♠8. This is right only if declarer's last three cards are such as ♠A J ◇10, when he will have to guess which finesse to take. Chagas threw the diamond queen from dummy. The ace of spades dropped the bare king and dummy's queen of spades won the thirteenth trick. Grand slam made!

The defenders knew, fairly soon, that declarer had started with seven hearts and three clubs. One of his remaining cards was known to be the spade ace. East knew too that declarer could not hold the spade king or the diamond king, otherwise the grand would be cold. If South held ♠A x ◇x or ♠A ◇x x, the grand would surely succeed on a diamond finesse. The only remaining case was that declarer held ♠A x x ◇–, when it would be essential for partner to retain a guard on the spade king. In the cold light of day, it seems that Mari should have thrown all three spades. This would make the position clear to his partner.

Mari's actual discards were ◇4, ♠4, then ◇2. If these could be relied on as true distributional cards, Chemla would know that declarer's shape was 3–7–0–3. However, many pairs do not signal their shape when defending a slam. They consider it more helpful to declarer than to partner. There was only one way to make the position absolutely clear – Mari had to throw all his spades.

On the next deal, from the Ireland–Iceland match in the 1991 European Championships in Killarney, both sides bid an apparently hopeless small slam in hearts. The Icelandic declarer romped home, aided by a defensive slip and a remarkable lie of the cards.

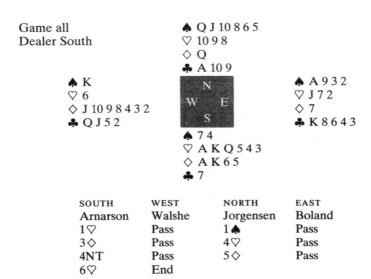

Game all
Dealer South

```
                    ♠ Q J 10 8 6 5
                    ♡ 10 9 8
                    ◇ Q
                    ♣ A 10 9
  ♠ K                                 ♠ A 9 3 2
  ♡ 6                                 ♡ J 7 2
  ◇ J 10 9 8 4 3 2                    ◇ 7
  ♣ Q J 5 2                           ♣ K 8 6 4 3
                    ♠ 7 4
                    ♡ A K Q 5 4 3
                    ◇ A K 6 5
                    ♣ 7
```

SOUTH	WEST	NORTH	EAST
Arnarson	Walshe	Jorgensen	Boland
1♡	Pass	1♠	Pass
3◇	Pass	4♡	Pass
4NT	Pass	5◇	Pass
6♡	End		

The Irish West led his singleton trump and the 10 won in the
dummy, East retaining his jack for a possible overruff in the diamond
suit. The situation looked hopeless but Arnarson called for dummy's
♠10. This is the sort of move players make when they hold a singleton
king and are hoping to slip past East's ace. Rory Boland rose with the
ace and was alarmed to see the king appear not from South but from
his partner. Normally, no damage would have been done, but West had
started with only one trump! Twelve tricks made.

Was it a mistake to play the spade ace? The actual situation was too
difficult to read. Rising with the ace would have beaten the contract if
South held ♠K ♡A K Q 5 4 3 ◇A J 6 5 2 ♣7, since East's ♠9 stops
the run of the spade suit. Against that, declarer would probably have
led a *low* spade from dummy if that were his hand. The position was
complex and I can't say I blame East too much. I am more inclined to
cast a reproachful eye on West's opening lead. A singleton trump?
Had he chosen a more orthodox diamond, or a club (the unbid suit),
declarer would have had no hope. At the other table a diamond was
led and the slam went one down.

We move now to the 1992 Vanderbilt semi-finals and a doubled
small slam in hearts:

East–West game
Dealer South

	♠ Q 10 7 5 2	
	♡ J 6	
	◇ A 8	
	♣ A K 6 5	

♠ 9 6		♠ A K J 8 4
♡ 10 7 5 2	N	♡ 3
◇ J 10 3 2	W E	◇ 9 7 5 4
♣ Q 9 4	S	♣ 10 8 2

	♠ 3	
	♡ A K Q 9 8 4	
	◇ K Q 6	
	♣ J 7 3	

SOUTH	WEST	NORTH	EAST
Chambers	Levin	Schermer	Weichsel
1♡	Pass	1♠	Pass
3♡	Pass	4♣	Pass
4◇	Pass	5◇	Pass
6♡	Pass	Pass	Dble
End			

Six Hearts was a fair slam because there was some chance of ruffing a long spade good. Peter Weichsel doubled not so much because he expected two spades to stand up, more because he feared that a minor-suit lead would assist declarer.

Bobby Levin duly led ♠9, covered by dummy's 10. Weichsel paused to consider his defence. How could he persuade declarer to ruff high on a spade return, perhaps promoting a trump trick for West? He opted for a double bluff, winning with the king of spades (rather than the jack) and returning ♠4. This is the sort of deceptive play that a defender might try when he did indeed hold six spades and wanted declarer to ruff low!

Unfortunately for Weichsel, Neil Chambers had a very likely club loser in his hand. When a low spade appeared at trick 2, Chambers discarded ♣3! West followed suit with the 6 and dummy's 7 won the trick. Fearing that West held all five trumps, Chambers crossed to his hand with the diamond king and ran ♡8. This manoeuvre, in fact unnecessary, proved successful too and the doubled slam was made. The slam was not bid at the other table. Had Weichsel won with a straightforward jack of spades at trick 1, he would have gained 11 IMPs, instead of losing 12.

Judging whether to cover an honour card can be more difficult than many players admit. Bermuda Bowl finalists (future champions, no less) have been known to go wrong.

Game all   ♠ Q 2
Dealer West   ♡ Q 9
                ◇ Q J 7 3
                ♣ Q J 9 6 3

♠ A J 7 5 4	♠ K 10 8 3
♡ J 10 5	♡ 8 7 4 3
◇ 10 5 4	◇ K 9 2
♣ 7 5	♣ 4 2

                ♠ 9 6
                ♡ A K 6 2
                ◇ A 8 6
                ♣ A K 10 8

SOUTH	WEST	NORTH	EAST
Aa	Muller	Groetheim	de Boer
–	Pass	Pass	Pass
1♣ (1)	Pass	1NT (2)	Pass
2♣ (3)	Pass	3♡ (4)	Pass
5♣	End		

(1) Strong club   (2) 8–11 points, balanced
(3) What is your shape?   (4) 2–2–4–5.

Norway faced the Netherlands in the final of the 1993 Bowl. Sensing that the Norwegians were bare in one of the majors, Muller made the fine lead of the spade ace against Five Clubs. East won the spade continuation and switched to a heart, which ran to the 10 and queen. Declarer drew trumps and called for dummy's queen of diamonds. Suppose you had been sitting East. Would you have covered?

De Boer chose not to cover. Mistake! The queen held the trick and declarer continued with a diamond to the ace. When the trumps were run, East was squeezed in the red suits. The game-going trick was made by South's ♡6. Had East covered the diamond queen, he would have transferred the guard in that suit to the West hand. No squeeze would have been possible. At the other table the Dutch North played in 3NT after a less scientific sequence. Helgemo (East) found the spade lead and that was 12 IMPs to Norway.

There was a strong element of humour on the next deal, from a Portugal–Iceland clash in the 1997 European Championships in Montecatini.

Love all
Dealer South

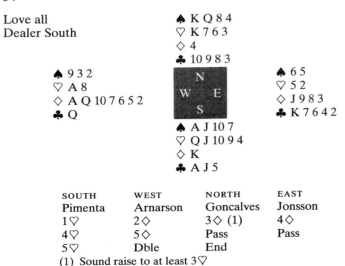

♠ K Q 8 4
♡ K 7 6 3
◇ 4
♣ 10 9 8 3

♠ 9 3 2
♡ A 8
◇ A Q 10 7 6 5 2
♣ Q

♠ 6 5
♡ 5 2
◇ J 9 8 3
♣ K 7 6 4 2

♠ A J 10 7
♡ Q J 10 9 4
◇ K
♣ A J 5

SOUTH	WEST	NORTH	EAST
Pimenta	Arnarson	Goncalves	Jonsson
1♡	2◇	3◇ (1)	4◇
4♡	5◇	Pass	Pass
5♡	Dble	End	

(1) Sound raise to at least 3♡

At the other table South had been allowed to play in 4♡, easily
made. The Icelanders did well to push North–South to the five-level,
but I don't admire that final double. There was every chance that one
or other opponent would be void in diamonds and East's raise to 4◇
hadn't promised any defence.

Can you foresee the defensive disaster that followed? West led his
singleton ♣Q to declarer's ace. He won the first round of trumps with
the ace, then attempted to cross to partner's ◇K for a club ruff. A
small flaw in this cunning plan emerged when East produced only a
diamond jack. Muttering 'Obrigado', the Portuguese declarer won
with the bare king, drew trumps, and eventually conceded a trick to the
king of clubs.

West had found the only defence to give declarer the contract. East
was favourite to hold the diamond king and there was a slice of bad
luck in the outcome. How could the disaster have been avoided?

A simple attitude signal at trick 1 would have been sufficient. If East
plays ♣7 (signalling attitude on an ace or queen lead), this will indicate
possession of the club king. West can now count three tricks for the
defence and there will be no need to risk an underlead in diamonds.

We end the chapter at the 1997 Bermuda Bowl, with Brazil facing
Norway.

Game all
Dealer West

```
                          ♠ 10 5 4 2
                          ♡ Q 10 7
                          ◇ K Q 2
                          ♣ A K J
        ♠ J 8 7                              ♠ Q 9 6
        ♡ A 9 6 4 3 2         N              ♡ K J 8
        ◇ 5              W         E          ◇ 8 7 6 4
        ♣ 5 4 2              S              ♣ 10 9 6
                          ♠ A K 3
                          ♡ 5
                          ◇ A J 10 9 3
                          ♣ Q 8 7 3
```

SOUTH	WEST	NORTH	EAST
Brogeland	Cintra	Saelensminde	P. P. Branco
–	Pass	1NT	Pass
2♣ (1)	Pass	2♠	Pass
3♣ (2)	Pass	3NT (3)	Pass
4◇	Pass	5♣	Pass
6◇	End		

(1) Stayman   (2) Shape enquiry   (3) 4–3–3–3 shape

The Norwegian North opened a 15–17 point 1NT, showed a 4–3–3–3 hand, then cue-bid in support of diamonds. Brogeland now bid the slam, although this seems an ambitious move on the information he had.

Cintra led ace of hearts and Pedro Paulo Branco signalled his enthusiasm with the jack! Can you believe it? A second heart went to the 10 and king, ruffed by declarer, and now there was a discard available for South's spade loser.

At the other table the Brazilian North–South pair also bid 6◇, receiving the heart ace lead. Helgemo restricted himself to the 8 from the East seat and that was 16 IMPs to Norway.

7. Disastrous High-Level Decisions

The opponents bid to Four Hearts and you sacrifice in Four Spades. If you go one down and discover that the heart game would also have failed by one trick, you have nothing much to worry about. Bidding is an uncertain science and that result is well within the acceptable margin. Now suppose you go 500 down in the spade sacrifice and find that Four Hearts would have gone 500 down too! Not so good. Either you or your partner has probably made a clear error of some sort. In this chapter we will look at some high-level decisions that were very wide of the mark. Our task will be to determine which player was at fault, thereby boosting our own accuracy in this important area.

We start at the 1964 World Bridge Olympiad, with Great Britain facing Italy in the semi-finals.

East–West game
Dealer West

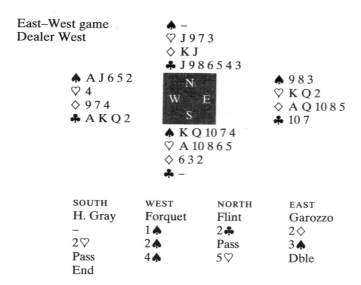

	♠ –	
	♡ J 9 7 3	
	◇ K J	
	♣ J 9 8 6 5 4 3	
♠ A J 6 5 2		♠ 9 8 3
♡ 4		♡ K Q 2
◇ 9 7 4		◇ A Q 10 8 5
♣ A K Q 2		♣ 10 7
	♠ K Q 10 7 4	
	♡ A 10 8 6 5	
	◇ 6 3 2	
	♣ –	

SOUTH	WEST	NORTH	EAST
H. Gray	Forquet	Flint	Garozzo
–	1♠	2♣	2◇
2♡	2♠	Pass	3♠
Pass	4♠	5♡	Dble
End			

Harrison Gray would have known what to do to 4♠ but Flint sacrificed ahead of him! The play went very favourably and Gray escaped for 300. This was still bad news when added to the 500 penalty suffered by Reese in 4♠ doubled at the other table.

Let's look at Flint's bidding first. The auction had ended 2♠ – 3♠ – 4♠, suggesting that the opponents had no values to spare.

Since trumps were breaking badly, there was every chance that the game would fail. Also, rather than guess what to do over 4♠, Flint might have shown his heart support on the previous round. He could then have left the final decision to his partner.

Nor was Harrison Gray blameless. I don't see much purpose in his 2♡ bid, on such a moderate suit. When you have a void in partner's suit, and a massive stack in the suit bid to your left, why contest the auction? Left to their own devices, the opponents are probably heading for a minus score.

Try the next decision for yourself. At Game All, you hold:

♠ K 8   ♡ Q 10 7 2   ◇ K 10 7 5 4   ♣ 8 5

SOUTH	WEST	NORTH	EAST
–	–	–	1◇
1♠	2◇	Pass	4♣
4♠	?		

Partner's 1◇ (Precision Club) shows either diamonds or a 11–13 balanced hand. What now? Pass, Double, or 5◇?

The deal arose in the 1981 Bermuda Bowl, played in Port Chester, New York. Indonesia faced Australia.

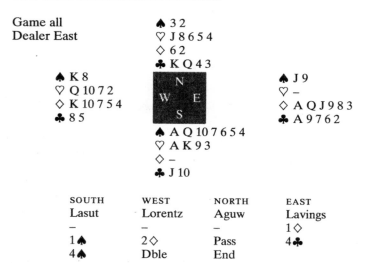

Game all
Dealer East

	♠ 3 2	
	♡ J 8 6 5 4	
	◇ 6 2	
	♣ K Q 4 3	

♠ K 8   ♠ J 9
♡ Q 10 7 2   ♡ –
◇ K 10 7 5 4   ◇ A Q J 9 8 3
♣ 8 5   ♣ A 9 7 6 2

♠ A Q 10 7 6 5 4
♡ A K 9 3
◇ –
♣ J 10

SOUTH	WEST	NORTH	EAST
Lasut	Lorentz	Aguw	Lavings
–	–	–	1◇
1♠	2◇	Pass	4♣
4♠	Dble	End	

Lorentz opted to double 4♠. A heart lead, giving East a ruff, would at least have beaten the contract since West would still score his queen of hearts. (East would hold up ♣A for one round to prevent a discard on that suit.) Lorentz preferred to lead a diamond and that was −790. Our main concern, however, is that East–West could have made 5♢ for +600.

What did you make of West's bidding? Initially he had to hold back a bit because partner might hold only a doubleton diamond. How should he re-assess the situation when he hears partner rebid 4♣ and right-hand opponent bid 4♠? Little weight should be placed on the fact that South bid only 1♠ on the first round. No-one forced him to rebid 4♠, vulnerable and contesting only a part-score. You can be sure that South will have close to nine tricks in his own hand.

Meanwhile, what are the prospects in diamonds? With a doubleton in partner's second suit, they are excellent. Partner would probably have rebid only 3♣ on a 5–5 hand. He is likely to have 6–5 shape. The diamond game will go one down at most and may well succeed. Even a Pass from West would have been good enough. Knowing of a 6–5 fit, East would surely have gone to 5♢ himself.

Another high-level decision for you. Sitting West at Love All, you hold these cards:

♠ K 6   ♡ J 7 5 3   ♢ A 10 6   ♣ A Q 6 3

The player in front of you opens a strong club and the auction unwinds in this fashion:

SOUTH	WEST	NORTH	EAST
1♣ (1)	Pass	1♢ (2)	3♡
4♠	?		

(1) Strong club
(2) Negative response, fewer than 8 points

What now? Will you pass, double 4♠, or press on to 5♡?

The situation arose in the 1975 Bermuda Bowl final, with (can you believe it?) Italy facing USA. This was the deal:

Love all   ♠ 10 3
Dealer South   ♡ Q 6
                            ◇ J 9 8 7 4 2
                            ♣ J 7 4

    ♠ K 6   ♠ 8 2
    ♡ J 7 5 3   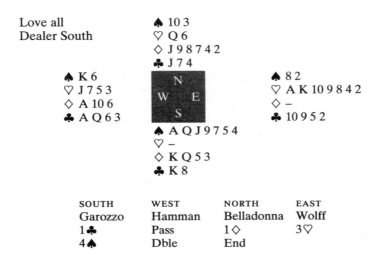   ♡ A K 10 9 8 4 2
    ◇ A 10 6   ◇ –
    ♣ A Q 6 3   ♣ 10 9 5 2

                            ♠ A Q J 9 7 5 4
                            ♡ –
                            ◇ K Q 5 3
                            ♣ K 8

SOUTH	WEST	NORTH	EAST
Garozzo	Hamman	Belladonna	Wolff
1♣	Pass	1◇	3♡
4♠	Dble	End	

An early diamond ruff or two would have beaten the contract.
Hamman naturally led a heart and the contract was made. The disaster
had occurred in the bidding, however. Five Hearts would have
succeeded on the East–West cards. Indeed, at the other table the
Italians made an overtrick in Four Hearts.

Trying not to be influenced by our knowledge of the whole hand,
let's assess the position from Hamman's side of the table. What is the
likely fate of 4♠? One down, seems a reasonable prediction. You will
probably make one trump and three tricks in the minors. If not, then
partner may come to the rescue with a trick somewhere. It is not
reasonable to hope for two down, since South had a 3♠ rebid
available. He was not forced to bid 4♠.

What are the prospects in 5♡, would you say? It's true that Wolff's
hand was unusually strong for a non-vulnerable overcall of 3♡. He
would have made the same bid on a weaker hand and Hamman made
allowance for this. Even so, West can hope that his hand will
contribute at least four tricks outside the trump suit. Add in six or
seven tricks from the trump suit and it is not impossible that partner
will make 5♡. Perhaps the most likely result is ten tricks for one down.

A point to remember on these hands is that if you bid 5♡ and go one
down, only to discover that 4♠ would also have gone one down, the
cost is not exorbitant. If you decline to bid on and they make 4♠, this
is really expensive. Even more so when you could actually have made
5♡.

We move now to a situation where psychology plays a part. You double the opponents at a high level and they redouble! What is your reaction? Do you consider a retreat or do you think they are bluffing, trying to persuade you to run? Some players feel that they should stand their ground as a matter of principle. It's true that a good player will not redouble unless he thinks he can punish any retreat.

Here is a particular example for you to judge. Sitting West, at Love All, you hold:

♠ 10 3   ♡ A 3   ◇ K Q 9 8 5 4 3 2   ♣ A

SOUTH	WEST	NORTH	EAST
–	–	–	5♣
5♠	Dble	Rdble	Pass
Pass	?		

Will you stick to your guns, or run to six of a minor?

The situation arose on this deal, from the final of the 1991 Venice Cup between USA and Austria:

Love all
Dealer East

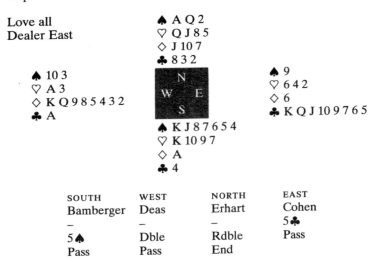

	♠ A Q 2		
	♡ Q J 8 5		
	◇ J 10 7		
	♣ 8 3 2		

♠ 10 3   ♠ 9
♡ A 3   ♡ 6 4 2
◇ K Q 9 8 5 4 3 2   ◇ 6
♣ A   ♣ K Q J 10 9 7 6 5

♠ K J 8 7 6 5 4
♡ K 10 9 7
◇ A
♣ 4

SOUTH	WEST	NORTH	EAST
Bamberger	Deas	Erhart	Cohen
–	–	–	5♣
5♠	Dble	Rdble	Pass
Pass	Pass	End	

Lynn Deas stood firm. The contract could not be beaten, however, and the Americans had discovered a new way to lose 1000. Had Deas run to 6♣, the cost would have been 300 at most.

West's initial double was questionable. The two aces would probably score, but a diamond trick was less certain. The most likely explanation for North's redouble (not in fact the actual reason) was that she was void in clubs or diamonds. On that basis 5♠ was surely a favourite to make. Meanwhile, what was the likely cost in 6♣? You *might* lose two spades, one heart and one diamond. Against that, partner might ruff a spade lead and make the contract, losing only to ◇A. The odds seem to favour a retreat.

When the same board was played in the Bermuda Bowl final, a similar situation arose. Balicki, West for Poland, judged excellently to bid an immediate 6♣. He was further rewarded when the Icelandic North took the push to 6♠, one down.

You're stressed out after so many high-level decisions? One more won't kill you. Vulnerable against not, you pass on these South cards: ♠K 5 2 ♡3 ◇J 9 6 5 4 2 ♣ 8 3 2.

What do you say after this start to the auction:

SOUTH	WEST	NORTH	EAST
Pass	3♡	Dble	4♡
?			

The situation arose on this deal from a 1981 Camrose international between England and Ireland:

North–South game
Dealer South

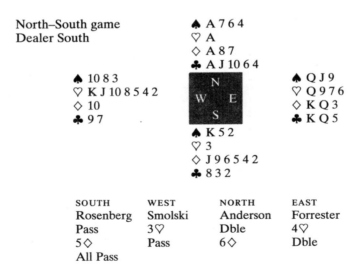

```
                    ♠ A 7 6 4
                    ♡ A
                    ◇ A 8 7
                    ♣ A J 10 6 4
  ♠ 10 8 3                           ♠ Q J 9
  ♡ K J 10 8 5 4 2                   ♡ Q 9 7 6
  ◇ 10                               ◇ K Q 3
  ♣ 9 7                              ♣ K Q 5
                    ♠ K 5 2
                    ♡ 3
                    ◇ J 9 6 5 4 2
                    ♣ 8 3 2
```

SOUTH	WEST	NORTH	EAST
Rosenberg	Smolski	Anderson	Forrester
Pass	3♡	Dble	4♡
5◇	Pass	6◇	Dble
All Pass			

Rosenberg bid 5◇, an action that looks quite wrong to me. David Huggett (South for England at the other table) found the same bid, passed out for 300. Here, the Irish North raised to 6◇, slightly bold but not at all unreasonable. Forrester ventured a double and, with the cards lying poorly and South well short of the values he should have held, the cost was a full 1100. All to save a game which would have failed by two tricks!

Ireland's loss was our gain – a valuable lesson indeed: do not save when vulnerable against not unless you think there may be some chance of actually making the contract.

We will end in a lighter vein, with one of the most amazing auctions ever to occur at world championship level. Hong Kong and Brazil, both strong contenders for a quarter-final berth, faced each other in the 1992 Olympiad.

North–South game
Dealer South

	♠ K 6 3 2	
	♡ K 6	
	◇ Q 10 3	
	♣ A Q J 4	
♠ –	N	♠ J 10 5
♡ Q 8 7 5 3 2	W　E	♡ J
◇ A J 9 8 6	S	◇ K 7 5 4 2
♣ 10 5		♣ 9 7 6 2
	♠ A Q 9 8 7 4	
	♡ A 10 9 4	
	◇ –	
	♣ K 8 3	

SOUTH	WEST	NORTH	EAST
Camacho	Chiu	Janz	Chun
1♠	3◇ (1)	3♡ (2)	3NT
4♠	Pass	Pass	5◇
5♠	Pass	Pass	6◇
6♠	Pass	Pass	7◇
Pass	Pass	7♠	End

(1) Showing both red suits
(2) Sound raise to at least 3 ♠

Chun's spoof 3NT seemed to have met with success when Camacho bid only 4♠ (why not 4◇ ?). However, he proceeded to hound the opponents all the way from the four-level to the seven-level, only to find that the grand was cold! What do you make of it all?

Chun's 5◇ bid seems reasonable to me. Having pushed the opponents to the five-level, however, he should have rested on his laurels. There were likely to be only 10 trumps between the East–West hands, so it was pressing too hard to advance to the 12-trick level. The likely penalty in 6 ♢ would not be far short, if at all, of the opponents' presumed 650 in 5 ♠. And if West held the heart ace Chun might have been swapping a plus score for a minus score.

His team-mates failed to shine on the replay:

SOUTH	WEST	NORTH	EAST
Yeung	Chagas	Chan	Branco
1 ♠	2 ♠ (1)	4 ♠	5 ♣ (2)
5 ♠	End		

(1) Michaels cue-bid, showing hearts and a minor
(2) To play in partner's minor

The Hong Kong pair failed to reach the slam level and it was 17 IMPs to Brazil. The blame here lies squarely with North. His 4 ♠ was a poor bid, suggesting a pre-emptive raise rather than one based on high cards. He should have cue-bid 3 ♡, as Janz had at the other table. There would then have been some chance of reaching Six Spades at least.

8. Rule-book Disasters

You will have gathered by now, if you didn't know it already, that there are many different ways to lose IMPs. One of the most aggravating is through the intervention of the Tournament Director, particularly if you don't agree with the ruling you get. In this chapter we will look at some rulings which caused vast numbers of IMPs to change hands. It is not our purpose to query the rulings. No doubt they were *perfectly* correct.

Looking at the unsurpassable record of the Blue Team, you might conclude that the Italian players of that time were bridge machines, ticking over with clinical precision. This is far from true. The late, great, Giorgio Belladonna sometimes made quite glaring errors, even mechanical errors such as not following suit.

The most famous of these was perpetrated during the 1959 World Championship. Italy faced USA (yes, it's true) and the match scores were almost level when this deal arose:

```
East–West game              ♠ K Q 7 3
Dealer West                 ♡ Q 8 3
                            ◇ Q 10 4
                            ♣ 10 5 4
        ♠ 10 5 4 2                          ♠ J 9 8 6
        ♡ A 10 9 7 4 2          N           ♡ J 5
        ◇ K J 2           W         E       ◇ A 9 8 6
        ♣ -                    S           ♣ K 7 6
                            ♠ A
                            ♡ K 6
                            ◇ 7 5 3
                            ♣ A Q J 9 8 3 2
```

SOUTH	WEST	NORTH	EAST
Belladonna	Harmon	Avarelli	Stakgold
–	Pass	Pass	Pass
1◇	1♡	1♠	1NT
3NT!	End		

In the Roman Club system an opening bid of 1♣ would have shown either a weak no-trump or a very strong hand. Belladonna therefore had to open 1◇. Can you believe his final bid of 3NT? Terence Reese, in his customary style, remarked that 'few players would think of such a bid and fewer still would make it.'

West led ♡7 against 3NT and Belladonna captured East's jack with the king. Even if West held the club king there were still fair prospects of making the game. Belladonna cashed the ace of clubs and played a second club to the 10. The American East allowed this card to hold. He won the third round of clubs with the king and returned his remaining heart.

How can the contract possibly have failed, you may be asking yourself. Did West win with the heart ace and switch to a low diamond, declarer rising with the queen? Surely not, since East's 1NT bid had promised fair values.

The answer is more horrible. When East returned his remaining heart Belladonna revoked, playing a diamond! West played the 9, thinking that he was maintaining communications with his partner, and dummy's queen won the trick. At this point Belladonna discovered that he still had a heart. The Director was called. Since the revoke had not been established, he ruled that South had to play his ♡6. West was allowed to take back his ♡9 but . . . dummy would still have to play the queen!

The USA West, Harmon, was not too proud to replace his 9 with the ace, snaffling the dummy's queen. He was then able to beat the contract by cashing the remainder of his heart suit. Belladonna was so upset by all this that he deliberately threw all his honour cards away, ensuring that he would score no further trick. He ended six down.

I recently discussed this ruling with the EBU's senior Director, Max Bavin, saying that I found it unduly harsh. At that time the ruling was correct, he told me. In 1987 Law 62C was added, section ii of which states: *After a non-offender so withdraws a card, the hand of the offending side next in rotation may withdraw its played card (which becomes a penalty card if the player is a defender)*. So, under today's rules, Belladonna could have retained the queen in dummy after West's change of play.

Well, we would all have been deprived of a great story! The rest of the set proved a nightmare for Belladonna and Avarelli. They went down several times, took a phantom sacrifice, and doubled the opponents into game. Carl'Alberto Perroux, the legendary Italian non-playing captain, had faith in his troops. Not only did he maintain the same line-up, he seated Belladonna and Avarelli against the same USA pair! He was amply rewarded when Giorgio had a terrific set, making a difficult slam and repeatedly applying the axe to collect some big numbers. The lost points were recovered with interest.

Moving swiftly on, we reach the 1965 (finger-signal allegation) Bermuda Bowl in Buenos Aires. Before the storm clouds broke, Great Britain faced USA on this board:

East–West game
Dealer South

```
                    ♠ K Q 10 7
                    ♡ Q J 4
                    ◇ A J 10 9 3
                    ♣ 5
  ♠ A 8 2                              ♠ J 9 6 5 4 3
  ♡ 7              N                   ♡ K 9 5
  ◇ Q 7         W     E                ◇ 6 2
  ♣ K Q J 10 9 7 2   S                 ♣ 6 4
                    ♠ –
                    ♡ A 10 8 6 3 2
                    ◇ K 8 5 4
                    ♣ A 8 3
```

SOUTH	WEST	NORTH	EAST
Leventritt	Rose	Schenken	Gray
1♡	3♣	3◇	Pass
5◇	Pass	5♡	Pass
6♡	End		

The British North–South, Reese and Schapiro had bid and made 6◇ at the other table. The Americans were therefore due for a small pick-up if Leventritt could bring home the heart slam. He won the club lead, ruffed a club, and ran the queen of trumps successfully. When he led the jack of trumps, Harrison Gray covered and declarer won with the ace. Both defenders followed to the king and ace of diamonds, at which point Leventritt claimed 13 tricks.

There was still a trump out! Since Leventritt had not stated in his claim that he would draw this trump, the Director ruled that he could not play on trumps while he had any other card to lead. Sympathetic as Harrison Gray must have felt, he declined to ruff until the *fourth* round of diamonds was played. Declarer ruffed the spade return and had to concede a club trick to West. That was one down and 14 IMPs away instead of a gain of 3.

A frequent cause for the cry of 'Director!' is the incorrect explanation of a conventional bid. A controversial case arose in the 1989 European Championships in Turku, with France facing Iceland.

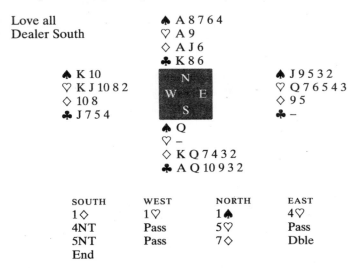

Love all
Dealer South

```
                    ♠ A 8 7 6 4
                    ♡ A 9
                    ◇ A J 6
                    ♣ K 8 6
    ♠ K 10                          ♠ J 9 5 3 2
    ♡ K J 10 8 2                    ♡ Q 7 6 5 4 3
    ◇ 10 8                          ◇ 9 5
    ♣ J 7 5 4                       ♣ —
                    ♠ Q
                    ♡ —
                    ◇ K Q 7 4 3 2
                    ♣ A Q 10 9 3 2
```

SOUTH	WEST	NORTH	EAST
1◇	1♡	1♠	4♡
4NT	Pass	5♡	Pass
5NT	Pass	7◇	Dble
End			

The Icelandic South's 4NT rebid showed a big minor two-suiter (most players would rebid in clubs when holding equal length in the suits). With four huge cards it was reasonable for North to head for a grand. He eventually chose 7◇, rather than 7NT, in case South held only five clubs and a bad club break would require the suit to be ruffed good. East doubled 7◇ and West duly led a club, ruffed by East. 100 to East–West.

The action was not yet over, however. Before his final pass, North had asked East the meaning of the double of 7◇ and had been told 'penalties'. North claimed that he would have removed to 7NT, had he been informed that the double was Lightner. Suppose you had been the hapless Director involved. What would your ruling have been?

The contract was amended to 7NT, making, and 27 IMPs changed hands (at the other table the French North–South had scored 940 in 6♣). The French were very unhappy about it. A contemporary report translated East's views as: 'North's question was unexpectedly strange and surprised me. Should it have been asked? A double of 7◇, that's just bridge! Did North perhaps want that I should how him my hand, and give him also my shirt and wallet?'

Directors, and committees, tend to lean in favour of the so-called 'non-offender' in these circumstances, even if there is a suspicion of sharpness in the air. Technically, the explanation of the double had been inadequate. Against that, North must surely have known that it was a Lightner Double and may have been seeking two bites at the cherry (7◇ and 7NT). If such tactics seem unfair, the only remedy is to answer questions accurately in the first place.

One of the semi-finals of the 1990 Rosenblum Cup was decided by an appeals committee. This was the board in question, with Canada facing Germany. It was played under intense time pressure, following repeated warnings for slow play.

East–West game
Dealer North

♠ 8
♡ J 10 7 5 4 2
◇ J 4 3
♣ 8 7 3

♠ K J 10 9
♡ A Q 3
◇ A 7 6
♣ K Q 2

♠ A Q 7 6 4 3
♡ 8
◇ K Q 8 5 2
♣ 5

♠ 5 2
♡ K 9 6
◇ 10 9
♣ A J 10 9 6 4

SOUTH	WEST	NORTH	EAST
Nippgen	Hobart	Rohowski	Kirr
–	–	2◇ (1)	2♠
Dble (2)	Rdble	3♡	3♠
4♣	4NT (3)	5♣	Dble (4)
End			

(1) Weak Two in one of the majors
(2) Asking partner to pass with spades, bid with hearts
(3) Roman Key-Card Blackwood for spades
(4) PODI: one or four key-cards

The Germans interfered heavily, not finding a single Pass on their first five opportunities despite a combined count of only 10 points! East's double of the 5♣ interference over Blackwood showed 1 or 4 key-cards. West mistakenly assumed 0 or 3 key-cards. Since this meant that two aces were missing and no slam would be possible, he decided to pass the double and defend the opponents' club contract.

East overtook the spade king lead with the ace and switched to his singleton heart. West claimed the queen and ace of hearts, then gave his partner a heart ruff. Three rounds of diamonds followed, declarer ruffing the third round. He ruffed a spade in dummy, then led a trump. When East showed out (having ruffed earlier), declarer conceded two more tricks in trumps. 'Eleven hundred,' said someone and the monitor wrote 1100 in the match record. In their personal scorecards all four players wrote that 6 tricks had been taken. Canada lost 8 IMPs on the board because at the other table the German East–West had bid and made Six Spades for +1430.

Germany eventually won the semi-final 154–151 and would face USA the next day in the final. In the middle of the night Canada's Arno Hobart was twisting and turning, unable to sleep. How awful to lose by just 3 IMPs! If only he hadn't mis-read that double of the Blackwood response. Or if they could have taken Five Clubs doubled six down instead of five down. He replayed the deal in his mind and – was he going mad? – surely the contract *had* gone six down! The defenders had scored one spade, two hearts, a heart ruff, two diamonds and two trump tricks. That was eight tricks for the defence. Six down in Five Clubs. There had been a scoring error. Had the correct score of 1400 been entered, the Canadians would have saved 7 IMPs and won the match by 4.

The conditions of the contest permitted an appeal, at any time before the start of the final (at 9.30am), on the grounds of a 'manifestly incorrect score'. The deal was reconstructed and Nippgen, the German declarer, agreed that he had in fact gone six down rather than five down. The Chief Director, Bill Schoder, ruled that the official score (five down for 1100) was not 'manifestly incorrect' but recommended the Canadians to appeal.

The appeals committee backed the Director's original decision, interpreting the phrase 'manifestly incorrect' as meaning such as a faulty addition of IMPs, 420 for a vulnerable major-suit game, or 500 for three down vulnerable. It did not include a review of how many tricks had been made. The German players were ushered from the appeals room to the table, where they faced and defeated an American team. Rohowski, at the age of 22, became the youngest world champion ever.

9. Disastrous Bidding Misunderstandings

Bidding misunderstandings happen in specific circumstances – sometimes in an undiscussed area of one of your own conventions, sometimes when you meet an unexpected convention from the opponents. It is in the nature of things that this chapter will be more entertaining than instructive. Even so, we may be able to draw a few useful conclusions.

Back in 1933 the steel magnate, Charles Schwab, donated the Schwab trophy to be awarded to the winners of a match between Great Britain and USA. Colonel Beasley, captain of the British team, found himself in a 'right pickle' (as they might have said at the time) on this deal:

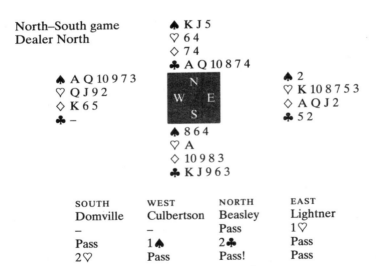

North–South game
Dealer North

```
              ♠ K J 5
              ♡ 6 4
              ◇ 7 4
              ♣ A Q 10 8 7 4
♠ A Q 10 9 7 3              ♠ 2
♡ Q J 9 2       N          ♡ K 10 8 7 5 3
◇ K 6 5      W     E        ◇ A Q J 2
♣ -             S          ♣ 5 2
              ♠ 8 6 4
              ♡ A
              ◇ 10 9 8 3
              ♣ K J 9 6 3
```

SOUTH	WEST	NORTH	EAST
Domville	Culbertson	Beasley	Lightner
–	–	Pass	1♡
Pass	1♠	2♣	Pass
2♡	Pass	Pass!	Pass

Nowadays most players are familiar with the idea of cue-bidding the opponents' suit, to indicate a sound raise. At the dawn of contract bridge such agreements had not yet hardened. Also, it was more common for players to make psychic openings – particularly when, as here, Lightner had opened at favourable vulnerability. Beasley's own shortage in hearts inclined him to the view that partner held length in the suit. He passed and Sir Guy Domville went seven down vulnerable, scoring only the trump ace!

Fortunately for us, the Colonel's view of the hand was recorded for posterity:

When I heard Domville's 2♡ bid – mark you, he had already passed – I had to guess one of two things. Either Lightner had opened on a short heart suit and Domville had something like seven to the Q J 10 and the ace of diamonds, or else he had no hearts and did not want me to be put off bidding game in clubs if Culbertson's bid was semi-psychic. The answer is that I should not have taken my guess then and there but should have made another bid to find out. If Domville did hold seven hearts, he could have rebid to three without much damage.

I have some sympathy for North's view of the affair. If psychic bids were then so prevalent that defenders had to reserve part of their system to deal with them, it would have made good sense to play 2♡ as natural and 2♠ as the fit-showing cue bid (South could not hold good spades or he would have overcalled). On the hand South actually held, 5-card support and only one good card outside, a direct club raise would have been more appropriate anyway.

When the board was replayed, this was the auction:

SOUTH	WEST	NORTH	EAST
Gottlieb	Morris	Jo C	Tabbush
–	–	Pass	Pass
Pass	1♠	Pass	3♡
Pass	5♡	Pass	6♡
End			

With Beasley's other pair bidding and making a slam, you may think that not much harm resulted from the misunderstanding at his table. However, in those days seven down vulnerable was not a mere trifle, costing 700, it was regarded almost on a par with wife-beating. Vulnerable undertricks cost 250 each and the penalty was a full 1750! No doubt Culbertson had this in mind when he found his smart pass over 2♡.

Don't assume that all bidding was hit-or-miss in the grand old days of bridge. Look at this superb auction from the Austrians, Frischauer and Herbert, facing USA in the final of the first ever world championship in 1937.

Love all
Dealer South

```
                    ♠ K 9 4 3
                    ♡ A 9
                    ♢ A 10 9 5 4 3 2
                    ♣ –
♠ 8                                    ♠ Q 5
♡ K Q 6 2           N                  ♡ J 10 7 4
♢ K 8 7          W     E               ♢ Q J
♣ Q J 4 3 2         S                  ♣ K 10 9 7 5
                    ♠ A J 10 7 6 2
                    ♡ 8 5 3
                    ♢ 6
                    ♣ A 8 6
```

SOUTH	WEST	NORTH	EAST
Frischauer	Vogelhofer	Herbert	Sobel
1♠	Pass	2♢	Pass
2♠	Pass	4♡ (1)	Pass
4♠ (2)	Pass	5♢ (3)	Pass
5NT (4)	Pass	7♠	End

(1) Asking bid in hearts   (2) No heart control
(3) Asking bid in diamonds   (4) Second-round diamond
control, and two aces

It was easy to set up dummy's diamonds and Frischauer made a grand slam on a combined total of just 20 points.

The disaster happened at the other table. Ely Culbertson, the inventor of asking bids, no less, had this auction with his wife, Josephine:

SOUTH	WEST	NORTH	EAST
Jo C	Schneider	Ely C	Jellinek
1♠	Pass	2♢	Pass
2♠	Pass	4♡	Pass
4♠	Pass	5♢	End

The same start, as you see, but when Culbertson made the second asking-bid, Jo read it as a sign-off and passed.

A contemporary description of Culbertson's asking bids states: '*A bid is an asking-bid if made at the four-level in an unbid suit. If no trump suit has been agreed, the last-named suit is agreed by inference.*' So, 4♡ agreed spades as trumps. The explanation continues in unhelpful fashion: '*After a positive response, asker may make a subsequent asking-bid in another suit.*' Here Jo Culbertson had given a negative response. Still, if this response had precluded a slam would

Ely not simply have passed 4♠? The situation was no doubt a rare one, although the Austrians clearly knew what they were doing at the other table.

Near the end of his life Culbertson stated that asking-bids had been his greatest technical achievement but his biggest psychological failure. Byzantine Blackwood, invented by England's Jack Marx, suffered a similar fate. It was greatly superior to ordinary Blackwood in a technical sense but, rated too complex by the populace, faded into oblivion.

Do you know when the Multi-coloured Two Diamonds made its debut? Terence Reese and Jeremy Flint unleashed the new weapon as long ago as the late Sixties. In the early days it caught many an expert pair unprepared. The numerous victims, it has to be said, included the inventors themselves.

On this deal, from the 1972 Olympiad, it was Garozzo and Forquet who ran into problems against the Multi.

East–West game
Dealer East

	♠ 8 5	
	♡ A K	
	◇ A Q 9 6 3	
	♣ K 10 5 2	
♠ 10 9 4 2		♠ K Q 6 3
♡ J 6 2	N	♡ Q 8 7 5 4 3
◇ J 8	W E	◇ 7 5
♣ J 8 7 4	S	♣ 6
	♠ A J 7	
	♡ 10 9	
	◇ K 10 4 2	
	♣ A Q 9 3	

SOUTH	WEST	NORTH	EAST
Garozzo	Cansino	Forquet	Flint
–	–	–	2◇ (1)
Dble	2♡ (2)	3♡	Pass
3NT	Pass	4♡	End

(1) Multi, weak two in a major or various strong hands
(2) To play, if partner's suit is hearts

Forquet responded to the double with a strength-showing cue-bid in hearts, or so he intended. Garozzo rebid 3NT to show a minimum double and a balanced hand. Forquet persisted with a second cue-bid, hoping partner would choose a minor suit. Garozzo now decided that perhaps partner held hearts after all. With a small slam makable in the minors, two of the world's greatest players had stopped in a 2–2 fit. The heart game went four down.

Who would you blame for this disaster? Twenty years later an illustrious panel in USA's *Bridge World* voted by 6 to 4 that Garozzo was more to blame. If North did hold long hearts he would surely start with a double of 2♡, to smoke out East's suit. Once East had bid 2♠, the North–South bidding would become easier. That said, there was widespread condemnation of Forquet's 4♡ bid, which put partner on the rack somewhat.

At the other table Rodrigue and Priday reached Six Clubs unopposed. Avarelli led ♠9 (Roman leads) which Rodrigue read as a short-suit lead. It was a false clue but it led him to guess the trump suit correctly. That was +920 and 15 IMPs to Great Britain.

Have you ever played a grand slam in a 3–2 fit? It happened to John Collings and Jonathan Cansino, playing for Great Britain against Germany in the 1965 European Championship. The cause of the disaster was a psyche, rather than a true bidding misunderstanding.

East–West game
Dealer West

	♠ Q 5 2	
	♡ 8 3	
	◇ Q 10 9 4 3	
	♣ 10 7 3	

♠ A K 9 3	N	♠ J 8 7 4
♡ K Q 10 2	W E	♡ A J 6 5 4
◇ A K 8 7 2	S	◇ J 5
♣ –		♣ J 9

	♠ 10 6	
	♡ 9 7	
	◇ 6	
	♣ A K Q 8 6 5 4 2	

SOUTH	WEST	NORTH	EAST
Collings	Deneke	Cansino	Chodziesner
–	2♣	Pass	2♡
4♠	5NT	7♠	Pass
Pass	Dble	End	

With the vulnerability in his favour, Collings psyched a 4♠ overcall. The German West had a massive fit in hearts and was now confident that there would be no spade losers. Willing to take a slight gamble on the diamond suit, he bid 5NT, asking partner how many of the three top trump honours he held.

What would you have bid now on those North cards? Cansino would have offered long odds against his spade queen being the setting trick against a heart grand! He went all the way to 7♠, doubled by West. The defence was not optimal. West cashed a top diamond and crossed to the ace of hearts for a club ruff. When West tried a cunning ♠9, Collings rose smartly with the queen and ruffed a diamond, adding a diamond trick near the end for 10 down. The penalty, even on the old scoring table, was still a weighty 1900. A loss of 14 IMPs, when compared with the less imaginative 7♣ sacrifice at the other table. The British non-playing captain stated that after such an irresponsible bid Collings would 'never again play for his country'. Was that fair, do you think?

It takes great courage to make such a psyche under the bright lights of a big championship. Had it goaded the Germans into a failing grand in hearts, everyone would have been talking about the 'bid of the tournament . . . Collings's brilliant 4♠ psyche'. The tactics that Collings favours must be judged in the long run. I recall another famous hand where he opened 3♣ on a 4-card suit: ♣A K Q 5. The opponents entered the auction and Collings's partner raised the pre-empt to 4♣ on three small clubs. Both opponents now looked favourably on their own holdings of three small clubs, bidding a slam. Collings doubled and cashed the first three tricks! I am pleased to report that little heed was paid to the npc's advice. John Collings is representing his country, with great distinction, at the time of writing!

Look now at Cansino's bidding. Are you happy with his leap to the seven-level? What could be lost by bidding just 6♠? He might have been doubled there (as it happens, allowing Collings to escape into clubs). If instead the opponents proceeded to the grand, he could reconsider the matter then, or allow the bid to run to partner for the final decision. The only justification for an immediate raise to 7♠ is that the opponents may then find it harder to judge the prospects of 7NT.

On to something different. Some pairs use 'fert' opening bids, where an opening of 1◇ (for example) shows 0–10 points. A Pass, rather than 1◇, would indicate opening-bid values. If such disruptive tactics were allowed in ordinary duplicate games, the general populace would soon stop playing the game. Why should they have to invent a whole new system, to describe all possible hands over a fert 1◇, when they would meet such openings only for the occasional 2-board round? Quite rightly, ferts are widely outlawed by national associations except at the highest level of play.

You might think that Bermuda Bowl contestants would have discussed in detail their countermeasures to fert openings. Not necessarily so, as this deal from the 1987 final shows:

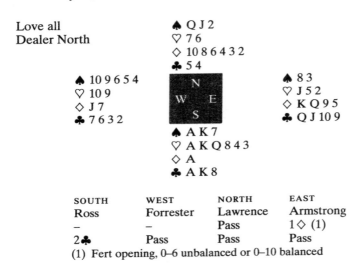

Love all
Dealer North

```
              ♠ Q J 2
              ♡ 7 6
              ◇ 10 8 6 4 3 2
              ♣ 5 4
♠ 10 9 6 5 4                    ♠ 8 3
♡ 10 9          N              ♡ J 5 2
◇ J 7      W         E         ◇ K Q 9 5
♣ 7 6 3 2       S              ♣ Q J 10 9
              ♠ A K 7
              ♡ A K Q 8 4 3
              ◇ A
              ♣ A K 8
```

SOUTH	WEST	NORTH	EAST
Ross	Forrester	Lawrence	Armstrong
–	–	Pass	1 ◇ (1)
2 ♣	Pass	Pass	Pass

(1) Fert opening, 0–6 unbalanced or 0–10 balanced

Mike Lawrence and Hugh Ross had agreed to 'ignore the fert whenever possible'. So, for example, 1 ♠ by South would have shown an opening bid of 1 ♠ rather than an overcall. The treatment of club hands had clearly not been discussed adequately. Lawrence assumed that his partner's 2 ♣ overcall was natural, rather than denoting a game-forcing hand, and the bid was passed out.

Ross won the heart lead, cashed a second heart to check that the suit was breaking, then played ace, king and another trump. A diamond switch at this stage would have beaten the contract. However, Armstrong apparently had no count on the trump suit. He played a fourth round of trumps, drawing Forrester's last trump, and declarer was able to claim eleven tricks.

At the other table Flint and Sheehan played the potential grand slam in 5♡, no doubt mightily relieved to gain 8 IMPs for their efforts.

When the contract is such as Four Clubs doubled, it is reassuring to have a 10-card trump fit. Particularly when it's the opponents who have declared the contract! It happened in the semi-finals of the 1989 Venice Cup in Perth, with Germany facing the Netherlands.

North–South game
Dealer East

```
              ♠ J 6 4 3
              ♡ A K 9 3
              ◇ Q 5 4 2
              ♣ J
♠ A Q 10 7                      ♠ K 9 8 5 2
♡ J                            ♡ 6
◇ K J                          ◇ 9 8 3
♣ K Q 9 7 5 4                  ♣ A 8 6 2
              ♠ —
              ♡ Q 10 8 7 5 4 2
              ◇ A 10 7 6
              ♣ 10 3
```

SOUTH	WEST	NORTH	EAST
von Arnim	van der Pas	Zenkel	Schippers
–	–	–	Pass
3♡ (1)	Dble (2)	4♣	Dble
End			

(1) Pre-empt in hearts, or long solid club suit
(2) Take-out double of hearts

Had West passed, a response of 4♣ by North would have asked South to pass if this was her suit, otherwise correct to 4♡. But . . . it had not been discussed whether this applied after a double from West (since North would then have the option of passing to allow South to define her hand).

Zenkel thought that she should bid 4♣ regardless. Indeed she was almost certain, from her own holdings, that South held clubs rather than hearts. East doubled and von Arnim took the view expressed above, that North would have passed to request definition. She passed, over East's double, and so did Zenkel. Had West led a trump, South could have been held to one trick for a penalty of 2600. When a spade was led, declarer scored two ruffs in her hand and the two red aces, going 1700 down. This killed a fine German board from the other table, where East–West had been allowed to play in 4♠ for 450.

Both interpretations of 4♣ would gather some support (von

Arnim's more than Zenkel's, perhaps). But once 4♣ had been doubled surely Zenkel should have reconsidered the matter. Was it still possible that partner held solid clubs? West had made a take-out double of 3♡ and must hold something in clubs. East had made a penalty double of 4♣. It was scarcely possible that South could nevertheless hold ♣A K Q x x x x.

The misunderstanding had a dramatic impact on the semi-final in question. The Germans had been leading by 30 IMPs or so with only 15 boards remaining. The momentum now changed and the Dutch eventually won by 21 IMPs. In a recent interview both Germans described it as the worst moment of their bridge careers. 'That board still gives me the creeps,' said Sabine Zenkel (now Auken).

Have you ever seen a deal where the same side played in Five Clubs doubled at one table, and Six Clubs doubled at the other? It happened in the 1992 Salsomaggiore Olympiad, during a match between Estonia and the Netherlands.

East–West game
Dealer West

♠ 3 2
♡ J 9 6 5 4 3
◇ 9 7 3 2
♣ 7

♠ K
♡ Q 10 8 7
◇ K 10 4
♣ Q 9 8 6 3

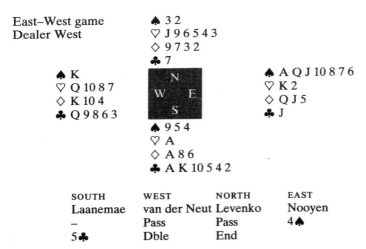

♠ A Q J 10 8 7 6
♡ K 2
◇ Q J 5
♣ J

♠ 9 5 4
♡ A
◇ A 8 6
♣ A K 10 5 4 2

SOUTH	WEST	NORTH	EAST
Laanemae	van der Neut	Levenko	Nooyen
–	Pass	Pass	4♠
5♣	Dble	End	

South's overcall was somewhat bold but there was an element of bad luck to it. Switch the West and North hands, for example, and the contract would have made with an overtrick. As the cards actually lay, the cost was a painful 1100. South met the same cruel fate at several other tables of the championship.

When the board was replayed, this remarkable auction occurred:

SOUTH	WEST	NORTH	EAST
Leufkens	Kobin	Westra	Suba
–	Pass	2♠ (1)	3♠
Pass	3NT	Pass	4♠
Dble	6♣!	Pass	Pass
Dble	End		

(1) Weak pre-empt in any suit

Six Clubs on a 5–1 fit. Can you guess what went wrong? A persistent series of email's to Estonia allowed Nikos Sarantakos to uncover the facts. The Estonian West had not seen the alert of the 2♠ opening! On the assumption that it was natural, he interpreted partner's 3♠ as a request to bid 3NT with a spade stop. This he duly did, rating his singleton king as adequate for the purpose. 3NT would have succeeded and so would partner's subsequent correction to 4♠, doubled by South.

However, Kobin was still under the impression that North's opening bid had shown long spades. In that case his partner's bids in the suit must indicate a very strong hand of some sort. Since he held a few useful cards himself, Kobin jumped to the six-level. He bid 6♣, assuming that East would correct if his bidding was based, say, on a powerful red two-suiter.

Leufkens assessed the South hand as a sound double of Six Clubs and his judgement was backed by 1400 in the plus column. That was a total of 2500 for the Dutch, a massive swing of 21 IMPs.

10. Disastrous Declarer Play

In this chapter we will inspect some deals where a big swing occurred due to cardplay. We must assess whether the declarers were unlucky or – it happens to us all – they mangled it.

Firmly in the latter category is a hand which won the 'Best Horror Story' award at the 1980 Junior European Championship

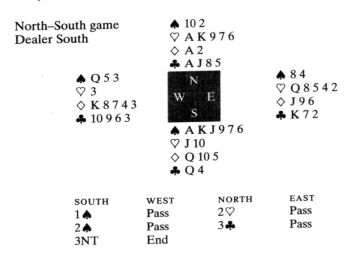

North–South game
Dealer South

SOUTH	WEST	NORTH	EAST
1♠	Pass	2♡	Pass
2♠	Pass	3♣	Pass
3NT	End		

West led ◇4, which ran to the jack and queen. The young declarer, Peter Splettstosser of Germany, surveyed the scene contentedly. There were tricks available from every quarter and it seemed it would hardly matter how he played the contract.

Declarer's first move was to lead the queen of clubs from hand. When this was not covered, he correctly assumed that East must hold the club king. He rose with dummy's ace of clubs and called for ♠10. The clubs were still protected and ten tricks would have been assured by running the spade 10. However, when it was not covered by the queen Splettstosser rose with the ace. He now led ♡J! Once again the honour was not covered, but this time declarer ran the card. The jack lost to the queen and East now cleared the diamond suit. When the hearts broke 5–1, a forlorn declarer found he had only eight tricks at his disposal. Such bad luck.

We now move up one notch, to the four-level. France faced USA during the 1974 Bermuda Bowl qualifying rounds.

Game all
Dealer South

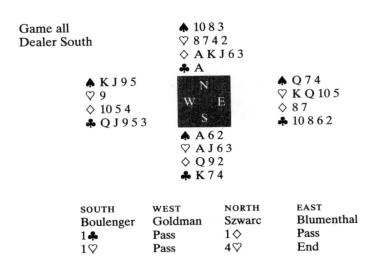

```
                    ♠ 10 8 3
                    ♡ 8 7 4 2
                    ◇ A K J 6 3
                    ♣ A
♠ K J 9 5                              ♠ Q 7 4
♡ 9                                    ♡ K Q 10 5
◇ 10 5 4            N                  ◇ 8 7
♣ Q J 9 5 3      W   E                 ♣ 10 8 6 2
                    S
                    ♠ A 6 2
                    ♡ A J 6 3
                    ◇ Q 9 2
                    ♣ K 7 4
```

SOUTH	WEST	NORTH	EAST
Boulenger	Goldman	Szwarc	Blumenthal
1♣	Pass	1◇	Pass
1♡	Pass	4♡	End

The 'prepared' 1♣ opening worked to the Frenchmen's disadvantage, persuading Goldman to lead the unbid suit – spades. Boulenger won with ♠A, crossed to ♣A and returned to ♡A to throw a spade on ♣K. He then played a second round of trumps from hand. Had the suit broken 3–2, he could have claimed the contract. As the cards lay, East was able to draw trumps and the defenders claimed the remainder. Six down, vulnerable.

Declarer does better if he crosses to the diamond ace and leads the second round of trumps from dummy. East can still beat the contract (by winning the trump lead and forcing dummy without first cashing another round of trumps), but the game goes only one down instead of six down.

At the other table, West led a club against the same contract. Hamman won in dummy and played a trump to the ace. He then ruffed a club and led a second trump, East winning with the queen. The French West may not have realised, but he had a critical discard to make. His choice was a 'useless' low club.

East knocked out declarer's club king and Hamman crossed to the ace of diamonds to lead dummy's last trump. East went in with the king and played a fourth club, declarer discarding. Had West retained his last club, he could now have forced Hamman's trump jack, establishing East's 10 of trumps as the setting trick. When he had to return a tame spade instead, Hamman made ten tricks – six more than Boulenger at the other table.

On to the quarter-finals of the 1996 Olympiad in Rhodes, with Indonesia facing Iceland. This spectacular hand arose:

East–West game
Dealer South

```
              ♠ J
              ♡ 10 9 8 7
              ◇ 7 6 3
              ♣ 9 8 6 5 2
♠ K Q 9 8 6 5              ♠ 7 2
♡ 6 4          N          ♡ Q J
◇ Q J 8 4 2  W   E        ◇ 10 9 5
♣ —            S          ♣ K J 10 7 4 3
              ♠ A 10 4 3
              ♡ A K 5 3 2
              ◇ A K
              ♣ A Q
```

SOUTH	WEST	NORTH	EAST
Thorb'sn	Manoppo	Baldursson	Lasut
1♣ (1)	1◇ (2)	Pass	Pass
Dble	2♠	3♣	Pass
3NT	Pass	Pass	Dble
Pass	Pass	4♣	Dble
Pass	Pass	4♡	Dble
Rdble	End		

(1) Strong club   (2) Diamonds/spades or clubs/hearts

I hope I'm not being unfair when I say that there was some truly awful bidding on this hand. I don't admire North's 3♣. Not only was he too weak to bid at all, he also had support for hearts – the other unbid suit. The removal of 3NT to 4♣ was an admission by North that he didn't have his previous bid. Now, the worst call of the lot. Just look at East's double of 4♣! He knew, from his partner's bids, that North–South had a giant fit in hearts. His delight at 4♣ as a final contract would have been better expressed by a pass.

West led ♠K against 4♡ redoubled, won with the ace. Had declarer now drawn two rounds of trumps, he would have made two overtricks for a score of – wait a moment – 1280. However, Thorbjornsson was worried that East might hold all four missing trumps. He ruffed a spade at trick 2, then took a club finesse. West ruffed and this was followed in quick time by a spade overruff, a second club ruff, and a further spade overruff. Declarer had lost four trump tricks where he might have lost none. One down! In another match Blakset of Denmark also went one down in 4♡, suffering the same cross-ruff. At other tables more than one North–South pair bid and made 6♡.

Was the Icelander's play unreasonable on the bidding? Suppose East had all four trumps, a hand such as: ♠7 2 ♡Q J 6 4 ◇10 5 ♣K J 10 7 4. Declarer can afford to cash ♡A at trick 2. He ruffs a spade, takes the club finesse (marked, on the bidding), and ruffs another spade. East is welcome to overruff with ♡J and return ♡Q, pinning dummy's 10 and promoting his own 6. Declarer will lose only two trumps and one, unruffed, spade.

Four Hearts redoubled is such a rare contract that you might think it could barely accommodate two play disasters at world championship level. Not true, unfortunately for some . . .

East–West game
Dealer West

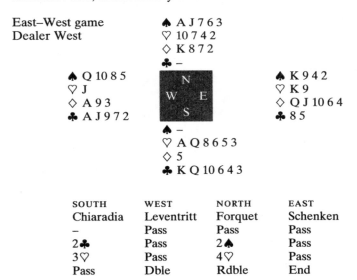

	♠ A J 7 6 3
	♡ 10 7 4 2
	♢ K 8 7 2
	♣ —

♠ Q 10 8 5		♠ K 9 4 2
♡ J		♡ K 9
♢ A 9 3		♢ Q J 10 6 4
♣ A J 9 7 2		♣ 8 5

	♠ —
	♡ A Q 8 6 5 3
	♢ 5
	♣ K Q 10 6 4 3

SOUTH	WEST	NORTH	EAST
Chiaradia	Leventritt	Forquet	Schenken
–	Pass	Pass	Pass
2♣	Pass	2♠	Pass
3♡	Pass	4♡	Pass
Pass	Dble	Rdble	End

Eugenio Chiaradia's opening bid showed 13–16 points and at least five clubs. His spade void gave him confidence, no doubt, that one of the other three players would keep the bidding alive. The heart game was reached and Peter Leventritt chose very much the wrong moment for a speculative double based on his stack in the club suit. Forquet let him know this with a prompt redouble and Leventritt led the ace and another diamond.

Chiaradia won the second diamond with dummy's king and cashed the spade ace, discarding two clubs meanwhile from the South hand. Without touching trumps, he embarked on a cross-ruff. Three spades were ruffed in the South hand and three clubs in the dummy. East overruffed the third club with the 9 and played another diamond. Fearful of an overruff and a trump return, Chiaradia ruffed with the ace, West in fact following suit. Now came declarer's last club, ruffed in the dummy and overruffed with the king. Another diamond from

East promoted West's bare jack of trumps. Incredibly, declarer had lost three trump tricks and was one down redoubled, losing 200. At the other table the US declarer was relieved to gain 4 IMPs for going one down in Six Hearts. Largely due to this hand, it is said, Chiaradia never again represented his country.

How bad was the chosen line of play? After West's double Chiaradia played on the assumption that the trumps were 3–0 offside. He planned to ruff all four remaining clubs, losing two trump tricks and the diamond ace. It seems the correct initial line to me. However, look at the position he reached after 8 tricks:

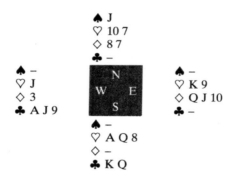

```
                    ♠ J
                    ♡ 10 7
                    ◇ 8 7
                    ♣ -
  ♠ -                                ♠ -
  ♡ J              N                 ♡ K 9
  ◇ 3          W       E             ◇ Q J 10
  ♣ A J 9           S                ♣ -
                    ♠ -
                    ♡ A Q 8
                    ◇ -
                    ♣ K Q
```

Declarer leads ♣K, not covered, and ruffs with the 7. East now shocks declarer by overruffing with the 9 and returning ◇Q. Easy to panic, but declarer must coolly re-assess the hand. West passed in first seat. Since he is now known to hold ♣A, and has already shown up with ◇A and ♠Q, he cannot hold ♡K. East holds this card, accompanied by no more than three diamonds. West must therefore have another diamond! Declarer should ruff with the 8 and exit with his last club, certain to score his A Q of trumps for the contract.

Time to step up one more rung, to the five-level. Back in 1930 a match was played between Great Britain (captained by Colonel Buller) and USA (captained by Ely Culbertson). The Americans won the match easily enough, despite an apparent card-play aberration by Culbertson on this deal.

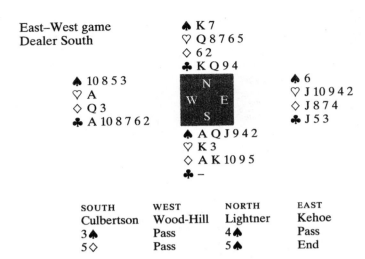

East–West game
Dealer South

♠ K 7
♡ Q 8 7 6 5
◇ 6 2
♣ K Q 9 4

♠ 10 8 5 3
♡ A
◇ Q 3
♣ A 10 8 7 6 2

N
W E
S

♠ 6
♡ J 10 9 4 2
◇ J 8 7 4
♣ J 5 3

♠ A Q J 9 4 2
♡ K 3
◇ A K 10 9 5
♣ —

SOUTH	WEST	NORTH	EAST
Culbertson	Wood-Hill	Lightner	Kehoe
3♠	Pass	4♠	Pass
5◇	Pass	5♠	End

In those bygone days a three-opening was strong. Ely Culbertson made one slam try, showing his second suit, and ground to a halt in 5♠. Do you see any way in which this contract might go down?

Dr Wood-Hill led his singleton ace of hearts and switched to a trump, won with the 9. Declarer has two reasonable lines now. He can draw trumps and play diamonds from the top, hoping for a 3–3 break or an honour to fall doubleton. A better shot would be to cash two top diamonds, ruff a diamond with the king, and return to hand with a club ruff to draw trumps. This line would succeed even when one defender held ◇Q J x x.

Both the suggested lines would have succeeded. At trick 3, however, Culbertson attempted to cash the king of hearts! West ruffed and returned a trump to the table's bare king. In desperation Ely now played a diamond to the 10 (although, of course, East would surely have split a holding of Q J x). When the diamond finesse lost to the queen, Culbertson ruffed the ace of clubs return and drew trumps. He had to surrender another trick in diamonds and went two down.

At the other table Colonel Buller played in Four Spades and was favoured by the ace of clubs lead, ruffed in the South hand. Two top diamonds stood up and a third diamond was ruffed by West's 8 and overruffed with the king. The Colonel discarded his two hearts on ♣K Q and ended with twelve tricks.

Ascending relentlessly, we have reached the small slam level. Norway's Tor Helness had an unfortunate experience, facing Switzerland in the 1993 European Championships.

North–South game ♠ A K Q 10 7 4
Dealer East ♡ J 10 9
  ◇ 8 4
  ♣ Q 6

♠ 9 8 2
♡ 2
◇ Q J 10 7
♣ K 9 8 5 3

♠ J 3
♡ 6 5 4 3
◇ 5 2
♣ A J 10 7 4

  ♠ 6 5
  ♡ A K Q 8 7
  ◇ A K 9 6 3
  ♣ 2

SOUTH	WEST	NORTH	EAST
Helness	Thompson	Helgemo	Aubry
–	–	–	Pass
1♡	Pass	1♠	3♣
3◇	5♣	5♡	Pass
6♡	End		

Aubry unleashed a weak jump overcall on a mere 5-card suit. This cavalier effort did not deter the Norwegians from bidding the good slam, but it was to have a decisive impact on the play.

West led ◇Q to declarer's ace. Tor Helness proceeded to draw trumps, noting that East held four of them. He then crossed to dummy with a spade and returned to ◇K. These comings and goings were not without purpose. Helness was attempting to count the East hand. So far he had shown up with one spade, four hearts and two diamonds. Add in six clubs for the weak jump overcall and all thirteen cards were accounted for. Concluding that East must have started with a singleton spade, Helness led a spade from his hand and finessed dummy's 10. The Swiss East won with the jack and declarer was now a cruel *four* down.

How would you have played the slam? With diamonds 4–2, twelve tricks can be made simply by ruffing a diamond, drawing trumps, and throwing the club loser on dummy's third top spade. If the spades aren't all good, you then give up a diamond to set up a long card in the suit. This line fails only when East holds a singleton diamond. Mind you, the chances of this are very much greater than the *a priori* odds, once West has indicated a sequence by leading the queen of diamonds (particularly when two rounds of trumps reveal East's 4-card holding in that suit). It seems that Helness cannot be blamed for his line of play.

Billy Eisenberg went down on this slam deal from the 1975 Bermuda Bowl. Some thought that he had played in somewhat 'unlucky expert' fashion. What do you make of it?

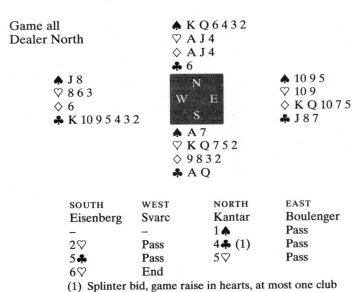

Game all
Dealer North

♠ K Q 6 4 3 2
♡ A J 4
◇ A J 4
♣ 6

♠ J 8　　　　　　　　　　　　♠ 10 9 5
♡ 8 6 3　　　　　　　　　　　♡ 10 9
◇ 6　　　　　　　　　　　　　◇ K Q 10 7 5
♣ K 10 9 5 4 3 2　　　　　　♣ J 8 7

♠ A 7
♡ K Q 7 5 2
◇ 9 8 3 2
♣ A Q

SOUTH	WEST	NORTH	EAST
Eisenberg	Svarc	Kantar	Boulenger
–	–	1♠	Pass
2♡	Pass	4♣ (1)	Pass
5♣	Pass	5♡	Pass
6♡	End		

(1) Splinter bid, game raise in hearts, at most one club

The Americans reached 6♡ and Svarc led his singleton diamond. The average club player would soon have recorded an overtrick, but Eisenberg was concerned that spades might break 4–1. In that case life would be awkward with the ace of diamonds removed as an entry. There seemed to be every chance that the lead was from such as ◇ K 10 7 6, in which case East would have to win with the queen if the diamond were ducked. The ace of diamonds would then be safe from attack and the contract proof against a 4–1 spade break. 'Play low,' said Eisenberg.

Boulenger won with the diamond 10 and gave his partner a diamond ruff. All the other declarers playing in hearts made 13 tricks (Belladonna/Garozzo were actually in the grand). However, at many tables North had made a cue-bid in diamonds, doubled by East. There was no temptation to run a diamond lead after that.

How do you assess Eisenberg's line? It's true that the diamond lead was more likely to be from K 10 or Q 10 than to be a singleton. However, to play low would gain only when the lead was from K 10 or Q 10 AND the spades were 4–1. Perhaps this tilts the balance in favour of rising with the diamond ace (particularly as declarer can still deal with a 4–1 spade break when the defender with the singleton spade has two trumps).

At the other table Lebel played in 6♠. The ◇K was led and when trumps broke 3–2 he made all the tricks, 17 IMPs to France.

We are now in the rarefied atmosphere of grand slam territory. The biggest swing of the 1997 Vanderbilt final occurred on this deal:

East–West game
Dealer South

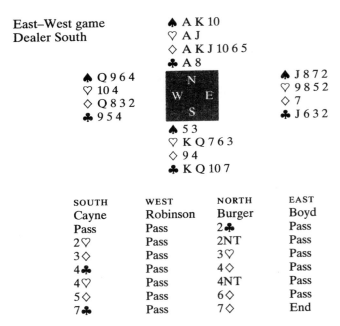

♠ A K 10
♡ A J
◇ A K J 10 6 5
♣ A 8

♠ Q 9 6 4
♡ 10 4
◇ Q 8 3 2
♣ 9 5 4

♠ J 8 7 2
♡ 9 8 5 2
◇ 7
♣ J 6 3 2

♠ 5 3
♡ K Q 7 6 3
◇ 9 4
♣ K Q 10 7

SOUTH	WEST	NORTH	EAST
Cayne	Robinson	Burger	Boyd
Pass	Pass	2♣	Pass
2♡	Pass	2NT	Pass
3◇	Pass	3♡	Pass
4♣	Pass	4◇	Pass
4♡	Pass	4NT	Pass
5◇	Pass	6◇	Pass
7♣	Pass	7◇	End

South showed five hearts with his 3◇ transfer bid, then at least four clubs. Call me a suspicious old gent, but the auction seems to have gone off the rails at this point. If Burger wanted to preserve the chance of playing in diamonds he should perhaps have rebid 3◇ rather than 2NT. Cayne eventually allowed diamonds to be trumps, but not until the seven-level had been reached. (7NT is a better grand since ♣J may fall in three rounds. At the other table declarer made an overtrick in 6NT by cashing the top cards in the minors; a double squeeze around spades produced a thirteenth trick.)

Against 7◇ Robinson led a spade, won in the dummy. Suppose you had been declarer. How would you have played the trump suit?

At trick 2 Cayne cashed the ace of trumps. When he crossed to ♣K and played a trump to the jack, the finesse succeeded but East showed out. He now had to lose a trump trick and went one down.

As Cayne would be the first to acknowledge, he did not make the percentage play in the trump suit. Cashing the ace first succeeds when East has a singleton queen; it loses four times as often when East has a singleton 8, 7, 3 or 2. Had Cayne played with the odds, finessing on the first round, he would have made his grand slam and swung 25 IMPs (+11 instead of −14).

We cannot be sure why one of America's top dummy players mishandled such a simple combination. The most likely explanation is that he was thinking back to the unsatisfactory auction, wondering whose fault it had been. Let that be the lesson we draw from the hand. Whenever an auction goes wrong and you end as declarer, wipe your mind clear and give the play the same degree of attention as you would normally. Easier said than done, of course! I have yet to master the technique myself, I admit.

Cayne does not hold the world record for IMPs lost on a piece of declarer play. The 1987 Bermuda Bowl was contested in Ocho Rios, Jamaica. Zaidie sat South for the home team on this deal, played against Canada:

Game all
Dealer South

	♠ A Q 6 2	
	♡ K Q 7	
	◇ 10 4	
	♣ A Q J 3	

♠ 10 8 7 4		♠ K 5
♡ 8		♡ 10 2
◇ K Q 9 6 5 2		◇ A 8 7 3
♣ 10 2		♣ 9 8 7 6 4

	♠ J 9 3	
	♡ A J 9 6 5 4 3	
	◇ J	
	♣ K 5	

SOUTH	WEST	NORTH	EAST
Zaidie	Schoenborn	Mahfood	Edgar
3♡	Pass	3♠	Pass
4♠	Pass	5♡	Pass
6♠	Pass	7♡	Dble
End			

At the other table the Canadian North–South pair had not distinguished themselves in the bidding. South's 3♡ was raised to 4♡ and twelve tricks were swiftly claimed.

Mahfood and Zaidie's disagreement as to whether 3♠ was natural or a cue-bid was resolved only at the seven-level. Expecting the spade king to score, if not the diamond ace, the Canadian East ventured a double. A diamond lead would have dispatched the grand slam to an early grave. However, West read the double as Lightner and (to cheers from the local VuGraph crowd) decided to lead a spade.

Zaidie was over the first hurdle when he rose with ♠A. To score thirteen tricks, he needed to throw two spades on dummy's clubs, then ruff out ♠K. The question was: how many rounds of trumps should he draw before cashing dummy's clubs? If he drew two rounds, he would need ♠K to fall in one ruff. If he drew only one round, he would succeed if ♠K succumbed to two ruffs. Against that, he would risk having the fourth round of clubs ruffed.

Either of these lines would have succeeded. Sadly Zaidie played on clubs without drawing any trumps. Groans from the VuGraph crowd! West ruffed the third club and played a spade to East's king. East now cashed ◇A for three down (a real sadist would have underled the ace to receive a spade ruff). That was −800 instead of the +2470. 17 IMPs lost instead of 18 gained.

11. Disastrous Opening Leads

Let's admit it, there is a fair amount of luck involved with the opening lead. The expert's edge is that he will put his finger on the right card more often than the non-expert. In this chapter we will place under the microscope some disastrously expensive choices made at the highest level. Sometimes there will be fault involved, sometimes not. It is for us to judge.

You will be better placed to criticise a disastrous opening lead if you avoid leading the same card yourself! Here are the leads we will discuss. As in the previous chapter, the hands are arranged in ascending order of contract.

1.

WEST	East–West game, dealer West			
♠ A 6 5 3	SOUTH	WEST	NORTH	EAST
♡ K Q 9 5 2	–	Pass	Pass	1 ♠
◇ 10 8 6 4	2NT	4 ♠	Pass	Pass
♣ –	5 ♣	Pass	Pass	Dble
	End			

South, with a marked two-suiter in the minors, has contested to the five level over your spade game. What will you lead?

2.

WEST	North–South game, dealer South			
♠ 9 7 6 3	SOUTH	WEST	NORTH	EAST
♡ K 9 8 6 2	6◇	Pass	Pass	Pass
◇ 9	End			
♣ A 9 2				

Not often you hear an opening bid at the six-level. What do you make of it? And what are you going to lead?

3.

WEST	Game all, dealer West			
♠ Q 5 4 2	SOUTH	WEST	NORTH	EAST
♡ 8 5	–	Pass	Pass	2 ♠ (1)
◇ A 8 4	6♡	End		
♣ Q J 4 2	(1) Weak two-suiter in the minors			

Equally rare is a six-level overcall. Any idea what to lead?

4.

WEST	North–South game, dealer North			
♠ 10 4 3	SOUTH	WEST	NORTH	EAST
♡ J 8 7 6 3	–	–	1♡	Pass
◇ 8 4	2♠	Pass	3◇	Pass
♣ Q 3 2	4♠	Pass	4NT	Pass
	5♠	Pass	6♠	Dble
	End			

South's 2♠ response showed good spades and around 7–11 points. His subsequent Roman Key-Card response showed two key-cards and the trump queen (probably ♠A K Q). What do you make of partner's double? Will it help you to find the winning lead?

5.

WEST	Game all, dealer East			
♠ K 2	SOUTH	WEST	NORTH	EAST
♡ 10 4 3 2	–	–	–	2♣
◇ J 4 2	4♠	5♣	5♠	5NT
♣ K 9 4 2	6♠	Dble	End	

Your partner's 2♣ opening showed 11–16 points with at least six clubs. What will you lead? Does that 5NT bid help at all?

6.

WEST	Game all, dealer North			
♠ 5 4 3	SOUTH	WEST	NORTH	EAST
♡ Q 10 3	–	–	1♠	Pass
◇ A K Q 9 6 2	2♣	3◇	3♡	5◇
♣ J	Dble	Pass	6♣	Pass
	Pass	6◇	Pass	Pass
	7♣	End		

Your diamond sacrifice has pushed the opponents from a small slam to a grand slam! What will you lead in this atmosphere-laden situation?

7.

WEST	Game all, dealer West			
♠ J 9 8 4 3 2	SOUTH	WEST	NORTH	EAST
♡ K 7 2	–	Pass	1♡	4◇
◇ 8 5 4	5♣	Pass	7♣	Dble
♣ 8	End			

After a brief but spectacular auction your partner doubles 7♣. You to lead.

8.
WEST	Love all, dealer North			
♠ 10 9	SOUTH	WEST	NORTH	EAST
♡ Q J 10 8 7 5 4 3 2	–	–	Pass	Pass
◇ 5 3	2♣	5♡	6♡	Pass
♣ –	7♠	End		

You are to lead against 7♠. Not such a difficult problem, really. You have a one-in-three chance instead of the usual one-in-four.

9.
WEST	Game all, dealer North			
♠ 10 8 6 2	SOUTH	WEST	NORTH	EAST
♡ 10 3	–	–	2♣	3♠
◇ 5 3	4NT	Pass	6♡	Pass
♣ J 10 9 8 7	7NT	Pass	Pass	Dble
	Rdble	End		

It seems that partner has the beating of the slam somewhere. Mind you, with the deal in a 'Famous Disasters' book, your opening lead may have something to do with it. What will it be?

On to the full deals, then. We start at the 1963 Bermuda Bowl final, fought between USA and Italy. The Americans had a healthy lead of some 40 IMPs when this board hit the table:

East–West game   ♠ J 7   (Hand 1)
Dealer West

```
East–West game        ♠ J 7                    (Hand 1)
Dealer West           ♡ A J 10 7 6 4
                      ◇ 3
                      ♣ J 8 6 2
      ♠ A 6 5 3            N            ♠ K 10 8 4 2
      ♡ K Q 9 5 2      W       E        ♡ 8 3
      ◇ 10 8 6 4           S            ◇ A J 2
      ♣ –                               ♣ K 10 5
                      ♠ Q 9
                      ♡ –
                      ◇ K Q 9 7 5
                      ♣ A Q 9 7 4 3
```

SOUTH	WEST	NORTH	EAST
Belladonna	Robinson	Pabis Ticci	Jordan
–	Pass	Pass	1♠
2NT	4♠	Pass	Pass
5♣	Pass	Pass	Dble
End			

The Americans would surely have made their spade game but Belladonna 'came again' with his 6–5 hand. He bid 5♣, rather than 4NT, to show that his clubs were longer. One down would have proved a fine sacrifice but the contract did not go down! Robinson led the king of hearts, won in the dummy, and away went one of declarer's spade losers. Belladonna now called for the jack of trumps (the correct card when missing K 10 x in the suit). He was soon able to ruff the diamonds good and pick up East's 10 of trumps with a second finesse. +550. At the other table the US North opened 3♡, passed out for −150. Italy gained 12 IMPs and eventually overtook the Americans to win the trophy.

What should West lead? South's minors were likely to be 5–6 and the lead would probably not matter if they were accompanied by two singletons. If South had a void heart, a heart lead would cost when dummy held the ace. If South had a void spade, a lead of the spade ace would not necessarily cost when dummy held the spade king. There might be no entry to dummy, to take a discard. This is one small pointer in favour of a spade lead. Against that, the East–West spade fit made it more likely that South would be void in spades rather than hearts. All in all, I can see no clear-cut reason to find the winning lead. Can you?

How often do you hear an opening bid at the six-level? Not often and the French West had to evaluate the situation carefully on this deal, from the 1992 Women's Olympiad in Salsomaggiore.

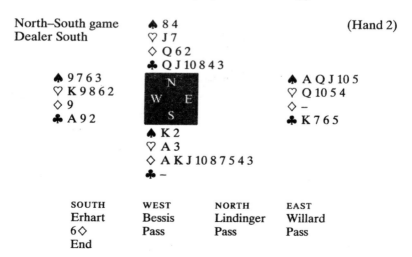

North–South game ♠ 8 4 (Hand 2)
Dealer South ♡ J 7
♢ Q 6 2
♣ Q J 10 8 4 3

♠ 9 7 6 3
♡ K 9 8 6 2
♢ 9
♣ A 9 2

♠ A Q J 10 5
♡ Q 10 5 4
♢ –
♣ K 7 6 5

♠ K 2
♡ A 3
♢ A K J 10 8 7 5 4 3
♣ –

SOUTH	WEST	NORTH	EAST
Erhart	Bessis	Lindinger	Willard
6♢	Pass	Pass	Pass
End			

Veronique Bessis led the only card in her hand that would permit the slam to be made – the ace of clubs. Maria Erhart ruffed in the South hand, crossed to the queen of trumps, and led the club queen. East did not cover and declarer threw her heart loser. Erhart eventually disposed of all three losers from the South hand, making an overtrick. At the other table South opened at the two level, allowing East to bid her spades. A spade lead beat 6◇ and Austria gained 16 IMPs.

What did you make of the lead chosen by Bessis? A player who opens at the six-level is unlikely to have two top losers in her hand. West could assume that South's club holding would be void, singleton, or king-high. In none of these cases was the lead of an ace likely to help much. It might save an overtrick, if a side suit in dummy would allow declarer to dispose of her club holding. It was unlikely to assist in beating the contract.

In addition, the lead of an ace is dangerous. It may set up the king in either declarer's hand or the dummy. It is particularly expensive when declarer is void and can ruff the lead, cross to dummy (usually in the trump suit), and take a discard on the established king.

The next deal is very similar. It arose in the 1989 World Junior Championships. Indeed, one look at the bidding will convince you that juniors were involved.

Game all	♠ J 10 8	(Hand 3)
Dealer West	♡ 9	
	◇ J 10 5 3	
	♣ A K 10 6 3	

♠ Q 5 4 2		♠ 9 7 6
♡ 8 5	N	♡ K
◇ A 8 4	W E	◇ K Q 9 7 6
♣ Q J 4 2	S	♣ 9 8 7 5

	♠ A K 3	
	♡ A Q J 10 7 6 4 3 2	
	◇ 2	
	♣ –	

SOUTH	WEST	NORTH	EAST
Stuart T	Damamme	Gerald T	Desrousseaux
–	Pass	Pass	2♠ (1)
6♡	End		

(1) Weak two-suiter in the minors

Alexis Damamme reached for ♣Q and Stuart Tredinnick helped himself to two quick discards. An overtrick resulted and Great Britain gained 13 IMPs instead of losing 13.

The lead of West's ace (dangerous, as we discussed previously) would have proved successful. The actual club lead demonstrated another risk – that dummy would hold the ace and declarer would be void, allowing a discard. A spade lead would have let the contract through, too. You will accuse me of being wise after the event, but I am rapidly coming to the conclusion that a *trump* is the best lead on this type of hand.

How often does the choice of lead against a suit slam make a difference of four tricks? It happened during the 1997 Bermuda Bowl in Tunisia's Hammamet. (The resort has happy memories for me. I met my wife Thelma there, some twenty-five years ago.)

North–South game	♠ 2		(Hand 4)
Dealer North	♡ A K Q 10 2		
	◇ 10 9 5 3		
	♣ A K J		

♠ 10 4 3	♠ J 9 6
♡ J 8 7 6 3	♡ 9 5 4
◇ 8 4	◇ A K Q 2
♣ Q 3 2	♣ 8 7 5

♠ A K Q 8 7 5
♡ –
◇ J 7 6
♣ 10 9 6 4

SOUTH	WEST	NORTH	EAST
Romanski	Ghose	Kowalski	Shivdasani
–	–	1♡	Pass
2♠ (1)	Pass	3◇	Pass
4♠	Pass	4NT	Pass
5♠	Pass	6♠	Dble
End			

(1) Good spades, 7–11 points

The Poles soared into 6♠ with three top diamond losers. Had this contract been passed out, West would doubtless have led a club – the unbid suit. In an effort to deflect his partner from this path, Jaggy Shivdasani essayed a Lightner Double.

Over to Santanu Ghose in the West seat. Was his partner void in hearts? Or did he have something good in diamonds? After long thought Ghose led . . . a heart! With the favourable lie of the cards declarer was then able to take all thirteen tricks for the unlikely score of +1860. Had Ghose chosen a diamond, the defenders would have claimed three diamond winners followed by a trump promotion. (At the other table the Indian contract of Four Spades was defeated in this way).

Do you blame Ghose for his heart lead? Fearing a club lead otherwise, East was entitled to make a Lightner Double when he held ◇ A K or ◇ A Q of diamonds. The hope would be that partner could judge from his own heart length that East could not be void in the suit. Unfortunately for the defenders, Ghose held as many as five hearts and it was therefore possible for East to be void. However, if the adverse hearts were 5–3 South might have shown his support. And if they were 6–2, North might have rebid 3♡ instead of 3◇. It seems to be a very close decision which red suit to lead. No doubt Ghose realised that at the time!

Another doubled spade slam arose at the US team trials for the 1996 Olympiad. Here it was the player on lead who doubled.

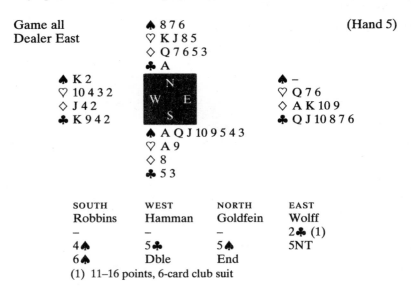

Game all   ♠ 8 7 6   (Hand 5)
Dealer East   ♡ K J 8 5
                ◇ Q 7 6 5 3
                ♣ A

♠ K 2   ♠ –
♡ 10 4 3 2   ♡ Q 7 6
◇ J 4 2   ◇ A K 10 9
♣ K 9 4 2   ♣ Q J 10 8 7 6

                ♠ A Q J 10 9 5 4 3
                ♡ A 9
                ◇ 8
                ♣ 5 3

SOUTH	WEST	NORTH	EAST
Robbins	Hamman	Goldfein	Wolff
–	–	–	2♣ (1)
4♠	5♣	5♠	5NT
6♠	Dble	End	

(1) 11–16 points, 6-card club suit

Hamman led a club, won on the table, and declarer played a trump to the ace, discovering that there was a trump loser. Had he chosen to finesse in hearts, hoping to establish a discard for his losing diamond, the club lead would have paid dividends – declarer would have gone two down, instead of one down on a diamond lead. However, Robbins could place West with a club honour and the spade king. East was therefore a strong favourite to hold the heart queen, to make up his opening bid. Also, with East's proclaimed length in the minors, the odds were good that his heart queen could be ruffed out. So it proved. Declarer eventually crossed to dummy with a club ruff and threw his diamond loser on the established $\heartsuit$J. Twelve tricks made.

Hamman may have paid insufficient attention to his partner's 5NT bid. It was the Unusual No-trump, yes, but to what purpose? It could hardly be suggesting that East–West sacrifice in diamonds rather than clubs, since a good fit had already been found. Wolff's intention was to suggest a diamond opening lead, in case the opponents took the push to Six Spades.

Surprising everyone, the Robbins team went on to beat its mighty opposition and represent USA at the 1996 Olympiad. There was no fairy-tale ending to the story. After a poor start in Rhodes, they failed to qualify for the knock-out stages.

We have reached the grand slam zone. The next deal arose in an England–Wales international in 1991 and it's possible that John Armstrong remembers the deal. He was sitting West.

Game all
Dealer North

(Hand 6)

		North		
		♠ A J 10 9 8		
		♡ A K 6 5 2		
		◇ –		
		♣ K 5 3		

West		East
♠ 5 4 3		♠ K Q 7
♡ Q 10 3		♡ 7 4
◇ A K Q 9 6 2		◇ J 10 8 7 5 4
♣ J		♣ 4 2

		South	
		♠ 6 2	
		♡ J 9 8	
		◇ 3	
		♣ A Q 10 9 8 7 6	

SOUTH	WEST	NORTH	EAST
Richards	Armstrong	Glubb	Kirby
–	–	1♠	Pass
2♣	3◇	3♡	5◇
Dble	Pass	6♣	Pass
Pass	6◇	Pass	Pass
7♣	End		

When North made a forcing pass over 6◇ South could place him with a void diamond, the king of trumps, and the major-suit aces. Hoping that one of the majors would provide enough supplementary tricks, he advanced to the grand.

Over to John Armstrong in the West seat. What should he lead? Knowing that all the major-suit strength would be over him, he tried a deceptive ♡10! His aim was to deter declarer from taking a finesse against the heart queen, should dummy contain ♡A K J x (x). The Welsh declarer saw that he needed to bring in the heart suit. It was barely possible that the opening lead was from ♡10 x x, so the contract appeared to be hopeless. 'Small, please,' he said, with a shrug of the shoulders.

East failed to produce the expected queen and a pleasantly bemused declarer soon had 13 tricks before him. Whether he would have guessed the hearts correctly on a neutral lead will never be known!

The Lightner Double, which is designed to make partner's lead against a slam easier, sometimes has the opposite effect. Rob Sheehan certainly thought so on this deal played against Uruguay in the 1980 Olympiad:

Game all	♠ Q 6 5	(Hand 7)
Dealer West	♡ A 9 8 4 3	
	◇ –	
	♣ A K Q J 6	

♠ J 9 8 4 3 2		♠ –
♡ K 7 2	N	♡ Q J 10 5
◇ 8 5 4	W E	◇ A K Q 9 7 6 3 2
♣ 8	S	♣ 2

♠ A K 10 7
♡ 6
◇ J 10
♣ 10 9 7 5 4 3

SOUTH	WEST	NORTH	EAST
Meyer	Sheehan	de Meyer	Flint
–	Pass	1♡	4◇
5♣	Pass	7♣	Dble
End			

Maria del Carmen Almeida de Meyer, North for Uruguay, leapt boldly to a grand slam at her second turn. Jeremy Flint's double was clearly Lightner, requesting a non-diamond lead. (In any case, it was clear from North's leap to 7♣ that there was no diamond trick to take.) Should Rob Sheehan lead a heart or a spade, do you think? A Lightner Double often asks for the lead of the suit first bid by the dummy. After long thought Sheehan led a heart. Flint clenched his teeth and the Uruguayans entered 2330 in their scorecards.

Was Sheehan unlucky, do you think, or was his reasoning at fault? If partner was void in hearts, the opponents would have a 10-card fit in the suit. It was possible for them to alight in clubs, with such a double fit, but would they not then run to hearts after a Lightner Double? I think so. In any case it was surely more likely that they had seven spades between them than ten hearts.

The British team fared poorly at the other table too. This was the auction:

SOUTH	WEST	NORTH	EAST
Forrester	Thalheimer	Smolski	Lerena
–	Pass	1♡	5◇
Dble	End		

Flint's 4◇ overcall had been decidedly timid (old-timers such as Priday and Rodrigue would use the word 'wet'). Lerena bid a more normal 5◇ and Forrester could do nothing but double. The contract did not even go down. He led a top spade, rather than his singleton heart, and declarer was able to ruff and draw trumps. When Smolski won the first heart he unaccountably returned a second spade, without cashing a top club. Dummy's club was thrown on the fourth heart and that meant an overtrick. The Uruguayans added a further 950 to the 2330 from the other table, swinging 22 IMPs their way.

We remain in the realm of Lightner Doubles, this time to consider what conclusions should be drawn when partner does *not* make such a double. The deal comes from a USA–Canada clash in the 1968 Ladies Olympiad.

Love all   ♠ 5 3   (Hand 8)
Dealer North   ♡ A 6
                 ♢ K J 10 7
                 ♣ Q 9 6 3 2

```
        ♠ 5 3
        ♡ A 6
        ♢ K J 10 7
        ♣ Q 9 6 3 2
♠ 10 9                        ♠ 8 6 2
♡ Q J 10 8 7 5 4 3 2   N      ♡ —
♢ 5 3                W   E    ♢ 9 8 6 4 2
♣ —                    S      ♣ K J 10 7 4
        ♠ A K Q J 7 4
        ♡ K 9
        ♢ A Q
        ♣ A 8 5
```

SOUTH	WEST	NORTH	EAST
Hayden	Begin	Hawes	Paul
–	–	Pass	Pass
2♣	5♡	6♡	Pass
7♠	End		

There were two reasons why the Canadian East did not make a Lightner Double of the spade grand. Firstly, the Americans might run into a making 7NT (cold, as you see). Secondly, most pairs play that a Lightner Double prohibits the lead of a suit bid by the partnership.

The Canadian West knew from the bidding that the opponents would hold first-round heart control. She perhaps expected partner to make a Lightner Double when void in hearts, because her eventual choice of lead was a diamond! Declarer wrapped up 13 tricks in quick time.

Most players would have led a heart from the West hand. The Canadian West may have attached weight to a piece of evidence we have not yet mentioned: East had not doubled the 6♡ cue-bid. Such a double should suggest a lead rather than a sacrifice. Had East doubled 6♡, then passed 7♠, she would surely have received the heart lead she wanted.

This was the bidding at the other table:

SOUTH	WEST	NORTH	EAST
Mark	Baron	O'Brien	Walsh
–	–	Pass	Pass
2♣	6♡	Pass	Pass
6♠	End		

Here West did lead a heart – the 2, to suggest a club return. East ruffed and returned a club, declarer rising with the ace and West ruffing. The contract now went four down, South scoring five tricks fewer than her counterpart at the other table.

The most expensive opening lead in bridge history arose in the Men's Pairs at the 1964 Summer Nationals, in Toronto. The players' names are lost in the mists of time, but this was the deal:

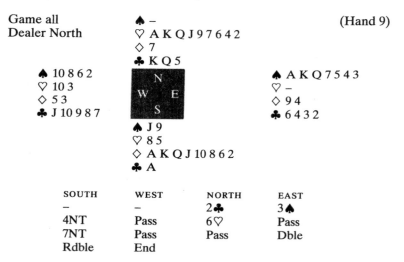

Game all   ♠ –　　　　　　　　　　　　　　　　　　　(Hand 9)
Dealer North   ♡ A K Q J 9 7 6 4 2
　　　　　　　　 ◇ 7
　　　　　　　　 ♣ K Q 5

　　♠ 10 8 6 2　　　　　　　　　　　　♠ A K Q 7 5 4 3
　　♡ 10 3　　　　　　　　　　　　　　♡ –
　　◇ 5 3　　　　　　　　　　　　　　 ◇ 9 4
　　♣ J 10 9 8 7　　　　　　　　　　　♣ 6 4 3 2

　　　　　　　　 ♠ J 9
　　　　　　　　 ♡ 8 5
　　　　　　　　 ◇ A K Q J 10 8 6 2
　　　　　　　　 ♣ A

SOUTH	WEST	NORTH	EAST
–	–	2♣	3♠
4NT	Pass	6♡	Pass
7NT	Pass	Pass	Dble
Rdble	End		

Not expecting South to have attempted 7NT without the ace of the suit the defenders had bid, and possibly attaching a lead-directional meaning to his partner's double, West led ♣J.

'They're all there now,' said South casually. 'Plus 2930, do you make it?'

At another table East–West sacrificed in 7♠ over 7♡. North–South took the push to 7NT, which was again doubled and redoubled. This time the defenders did find the spade lead. West remembered to unblock the 10 and 8 and that was seven down for 4000. A net swing of 6930, just on the opening lead.

Mind you, it was slightly easier for the defenders at the second table. East was on lead!

12. Disastrous Slam Bidding

In this chapter we will look at some auctions, mainly unopposed, where top-class players either failed to reach a cold slam or bid one that had no play. As always, we must assess whether the players were unlucky or someone made a clear-cut error.

'We start at the beginning,' as the story-tellers say. This deal from the 1931 Culbertson–Lenz match has passed into posterity.

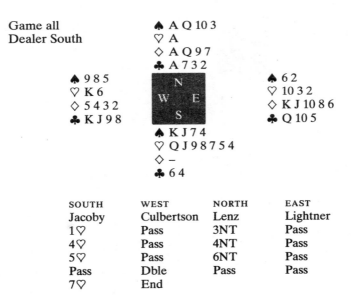

Game all
Dealer South

	♠ A Q 10 3	
	♡ A	
	◇ A Q 9 7	
	♣ A 7 3 2	

♠ 9 8 5		♠ 6 2
♡ K 6		♡ 10 3 2
◇ 5 4 3 2		◇ K J 10 8 6
♣ K J 9 8		♣ Q 10 5

	♠ K J 7 4
	♡ Q J 9 8 7 5 4
	◇ –
	♣ 6 4

SOUTH	WEST	NORTH	EAST
Jacoby	Culbertson	Lenz	Lightner
1♡	Pass	3NT	Pass
4♡	Pass	4NT	Pass
5♡	Pass	6NT	Pass
Pass	Dble	Pass	Pass
7♡	End		

All these big names were masterful cardplayers, but what awful bidding! It would be laughed out of court nowadays, even in a beginners' game. Who should take the lion's share of the blame, do you think? There was no chance of finding the spade fit (7♠ was cold), once Lenz had replied 3NT. Given that, should Lenz have bid 6♡ or 6NT? It is said that his four aces, and an upbringing in Auction Bridge, urged him towards no-trumps. It's true also that he did have two A Q tenaces to protect.

Jacoby's opening bid of 1♡ had little to commend it but his worst bid was surely the pull of 6NT to 7♡. Prospects of the heart grand succeeding were negligible. Had 6NT doubled been allowed to stand,

East might well not have found the club lead necessary to beat the slam. I am going to assign the blame:

Jacoby 60%   Lenz 40%   Bad luck 0%

In his report of the match Culbertson warmly congratulated himself on his brilliant psychology in doubling 6NT. Yes, compared with most of the calls made, it was a fine effort. Lenz and Jacoby had a prolonged argument over the deal, and on various others that followed. Eventually Jacoby could take no more and withdrew after the 101st rubber.

A few years later, in 1937, USA faced Austria in a world championship match. Both Ely and Jo Culbertson underbid on this deal:

Love all
Dealer South

```
                        ♠ A 4
                        ♡ K 10 4
                        ◇ A
                        ♣ A 8 7 5 4 3 2
        ♠ 9 8                              ♠ Q 10 7 5 3
        ♡ J 8 7 6 5 3          N           ♡ Q
        ◇ K 10 6 3        W         E      ◇ Q 8 7 4 2
        ♣ J                   S           ♣ Q 6
                        ♠ K J 6 2
                        ♡ A 9 2
                        ◇ J 9 5
                        ♣ K 10 9
```

SOUTH	WEST	NORTH	EAST
Ely C	Jellinek	Jo C	Schneider
Pass	Pass	1♣	Pass
1♠	Pass	2♣	Pass
2NT	Pass	3NT	End

Six Clubs was cold if clubs were 2–1. If they were not 2–1, a diamond lead would put even 3NT at risk. Who was to blame? Three of the calls were on the cautious side (the initial Pass by South, the 2♣ rebid, and the 2NT rebid). Of these I would single out Mrs Culbertson's 2♣ as the culprit. With seven clubs, 15 points, and two side aces, she would need very little opposite to make 3NT (♣ K x x would be enough). She was surely worth a jump rebid of 3♣.

The blame allocation? Undue chivalry towards women would be out of place in a technical work such as this. I'll make it:

Ely Culbertson 10%   Jo Culbertson 75%   Bad luck 15%

At the other table the Austrians displayed no such reticence! This was their auction:

SOUTH	WEST	NORTH	EAST
Herbert	Sobel	Frischauer	Vogelhofer
1♣	Pass	1NT	Pass
2NT	Pass	3♣	Pass
3♠	Pass	4♣	Pass
5♣	Pass	7♣	End

North's 1NT response was forcing and the 2NT rebid showed no extra values. North deemed the 3♠ and 5♣ continuations as sufficiently encouraging to bid the grand. Helen Sobel led a heart to the queen and ace. After failing to ruff out the queen of spades, declarer took a successful finesse against the heart jack. Thirteen tricks and a huge swing to the Austrian team, who went on to win the match.

In the 1980 Lederer Memorial Trophy Reese and Schapiro suffered the same fate as the Culbertsons. They reached only the game level when a grand slam could have been made.

Game all
Dealer South

	♠ A 10	
	♡ Q 10 9 8 6 3	
	◇ A 3	
	♣ 9 8 3	

♠ Q 8 6 5		♠ J 9 7 2
♡ –		♡ K
◇ J 8 5 4		◇ Q 9 7 6
♣ Q J 7 6 2		♣ K 10 5 4

	♠ K 4 3	
	♡ A J 7 5 4 2	
	◇ K 10 2	
	♣ A	

SOUTH	WEST	NORTH	EAST
Reese	Coyle	Schapiro	Silverstone
1♡	Pass	2◇	Pass
3♡	Pass	3♠	Pass
4◇	Pass	4♡	End

Schapiro, with no Swiss-type response available, had to invent a 2◇ response. Over Reese's informative 3♡ rebid he continued with 3♠, natural on the face of it although subsequent actions might indicate that it had been an advance cue-bid. Reese gave preference to diamonds and Schapiro now showed his heart support. The auction died in 4♡ and it is not difficult to imagine the reactions of the South player as dummy appeared!

Who was to blame? As I see it, Schapiro did not complete the description of his hand. He might have held a doubleton heart on that sequence. Had Schapiro bid 5♡ instead of 4♡ at his third turn, it would have been obvious that he held good heart support and that 3♠ had been an advance cue-bid.

Should we allocate any blame to Reese, on the grounds that partner would have bid 4♡ directly (rather than 3♡) if he had no slam ambitions? I don't believe so. From Reese's point of view Schapiro might have been angling for a game in no-trumps.

Reese 0%   Schapiro 85%   Bad luck 15%

Moving swiftly on, we look next at an instructive deal from a 1993 Camrose international between England and Wales.

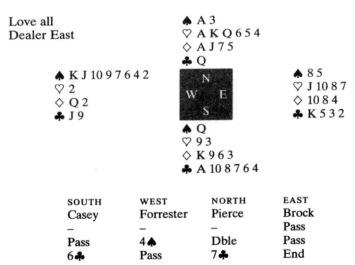

Love all
Dealer East

	♠ A 3	
	♡ A K Q 6 5 4	
	◇ A J 7 5	
	♣ Q	

♠ K J 10 9 7 6 4 2		♠ 8 5
♡ 2		♡ J 10 8 7
◇ Q 2		◇ 10 8 4
♣ J 9		♣ K 5 3 2

	♠ Q	
	♡ 9 3	
	◇ K 9 6 3	
	♣ A 10 8 7 6 4	

SOUTH	WEST	NORTH	EAST
Casey	Forrester	Pierce	Brock
–	–	–	Pass
Pass	4♠	Dble	Pass
6♣	Pass	7♣	End

The inglorious club grand went one down. At the other table West opened only 3♠ and North's 3NT ended the auction for +460. Had the Welsh North passed 6♣, a fortunate swing would have come his way. Even if West leads his singleton heart there is no defence. Declarer wins in the dummy and advances the queen of trumps, giving East no winning option. A correction to 6♡ would also have been successful.

Who was to blame? South's 6♣ was excessive. The point to remember, after a high opening such as 4♠, is that responder will usually pass out the double with a poor hand. He needs a long suit and fair values to attempt 11 tricks, playing the hand, rather than 4 in defence. Had South bid 5♣, instead of 6♣, North would have expected roughly what South held. That said, North's raise to the grand was ambitious too. Do you see why? South was a passed hand! With a suit as good as ♣A K J x x x he might well have opened a non-vulnerable pre-empt. Let's make it:

Casey 70%   Pierce 25%   Bad luck 5%

One of the best TV bridge series was 'Grand Slam', back in 1981. Great Britain (Flint/Rodrigue, Davies/Gardener) took on USA (Granovetter/Silverman, Moss/Mitchell). Have the contestants' many excellent plays stuck in the mind? I'm afraid not. The deal that everyone remembers is, appropriately in the circumstances, this spectacular Grand Slam disaster:

```
Love all              ♠ A 10 5
Dealer West           ♡ A K J 8 6 2
                      ◇ K
                      ♣ 6 5 4
        ♠ K Q 6 2          N          ♠ J 9 8 3
        ♡ 7 4                          ♡ –
        ◇ Q J 8 5 4 2   W     E        ◇ A 10 9 7 6 3
        ♣ 8                  S         ♣ Q J 3
                      ♠ 7 4
                      ♡ Q 10 9 5 3
                      ◇ –
                      ♣ A K 10 9 7 2
```

SOUTH	WEST	NORTH	EAST
Gardener	Moss	Davies	Mitchell
–	Pass	1♡	Pass
3♣	Dble	3♡	4♠
5◇	Pass	5♠	Pass
5NT	Pass	7♣	Pass
7♡	Pass	Pass	7♠
Dble	Pass	7NT	Dble
End			

Nicola Gardener's 5NT asked partner to bid a grand if she held two of the three top trump honours. Many expert partnerships agree to respond 7♣, rather than seven of the supposed trump suit, when they hold the required honours. This allows partner to choose some other denomination for the grand slam. On this auction, for example, South might want to play in 7♣ if she held solid clubs and only Q x x in hearts.

Declarer would have needed an inspired view of the club suit to make 7♡. However, the Americans sacrificed in 7♠, setting the British pair a problem of a different sort. Gardener doubled, expressing the view that 7NT would not be a success. Davies was not so certain. The hearts and clubs were probably running, otherwise 7♡ would not have been a make. If that were the case, the only remaining problem in 7NT was that South's first-round diamond control was a void, rather than the ace. There were two reasons why it was unlikely that South had a diamond void. Her jump shift had suggested a high point-count; also, the Americans had contested in spades rather than diamonds and were therefore unlikely to hold twelve diamonds between them. 'Seven no-trumps,' said Pat Davies.

Jacqui Mitchell doubled and, having checked that it was her lead, placed ♢A on the table. Had the British pair noticed that it was not in fact East's lead(!), they could in theory have barred the lead, taken the right view of clubs and . . . made the doubled grand slam. None of these possibilities came to pass and 7NT went an embarrassing 1100 down. At the other table Jeremy Flint was 300 down in his 7♢ sacrifice. 16 IMPs away.

How shall we allocate the blame for this 7NT contract? I'm not a great fan of the initial jump shift on only 9 points. If you start with 2♣ you will hear a more descriptive rebid from partner and can bid as strongly as you like thereafter. The main cause of Davies's eventual misjudgement was her expectation of more points from the South hand. Against that, there must be some reason why Gardener had doubled 7♠ rather than make a forcing pass. If she did hold the cards that Davies needed, would she not have been happy to invite 7NT?

I'm a controversial old devil, am I not? Ignoring David Gostyn's advice to give 100% of the blame to Pat Davies, I'm going to make it:

Gardener 40%   Davies 40%   Bad luck 20%

13. It Cost Us the Championship

You or your team-mates have a terrible board and lose 15 IMPs. It doesn't really matter if you still win the match, does it? You can have a good laugh about it as you sink a celebratory pint. The really painful disasters are those that cost a vital match or championship. In this final chapter we will look at some of the most costly bids and plays ever made at the bridge table – the sort that will haunt the perpetrators until their dying days.

First, a bidding problem for you. Sitting West, against vulnerable opponents, you hold:

♠ 9 7 3　　♡ K J 10 9 7 4　　◇ 5　　♣ J 10 7

SOUTH	WEST	NORTH	EAST
–	–	1NT (1)	2♣ (2)
2NT (3)	4♡	Pass	Pass
5◇	?		

(1) Strong no-trump, 16–18 points
(2) Showing both majors
(3) Game-forcing, asking for further information

What now? Will you take the push to 5♡ or hope that three tricks can be found in defence? A secondary question: if you decide to pass and partner doubles the diamond game, what will you lead?

The problem was originally faced by Michel Lebel, playing for France against USA in the semi-finals of the 1975 Bermuda Bowl. This was the deal:

North–South game
Dealer North

			♠ K 6			
			♡ Q 3			
			◇ A Q J			
			♣ A 9 8 6 3 2			

♠ 9 7 3
♡ K J 10 9 7 4
◇ 5
♣ J 10 7

♠ A Q J 10 4
♡ A 8 6 5 2
◇ 3
♣ 5 4

♠ 8 5 2
♡ –
◇ K 10 9 8 7 6 4 2
♣ K Q

SOUTH	WEST	NORTH	EAST
Hamman	Lebel	Wolff	Mari
–	–	1NT	2♣
2NT	4♡	Pass	Pass
5◇	Pass	Pass	Dble
End			

Lebel passed Hamman's 5◇ bid, Mari doubling on the way out. Lebel duly found the best lead of a spade but this served only to prevent overtricks. Hamman collected +750 as a reward for his 2NT bid, cunningly masking his extreme distribution.

If Lebel had bid 5♡, he would have gone only one down. Some indications were present that this was the correct action. North–South were known to have a big double fit in the minors. West himself had no defence at all to 5◇. Indeed, his extreme length in hearts was a negative factor. It might kill the chance of partner scoring the heart ace.

There was another reason in favour of bidding 5♡. One or other opponent might advance to 6◇. Unlikely, you say? It's exactly what did happen at the other table:

SOUTH	WEST	NORTH	EAST
Boulenger	Kantar	Svarc	Eisenberg
–	–	1NT	2♣
5◇	5♡	Pass	Pass
6◇	Pass	Pass	Dble
End			

Eddie Kantar, West, found the crucial spade lead and that was 14
IMPs to the USA (200 plus 750). The Americans' eventual margin of
victory was just 12 IMPs.

Another opening lead problem for you. Sitting West, vulnerable
against not, you hold:

♠ Q 10 9 6 5 3　　♡ A 10 6 4 2　　◇ 5　　♣ 6

SOUTH	WEST	NORTH	EAST
–	–	–	1♡
2♡ (1)	4♡	5NT	Pass
6◇	Pass	Pass	Dble
End			

(1)　Michaels cue-bid, spades and a minor

What do you make of partner's double? What will you lead? Also,
suppose partner had not doubled the slam. Would you have led
something different? The deal arose in the final of the 1993 Spring
Foursomes, in England. This was the full layout:

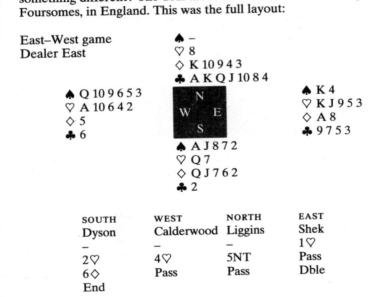

East–West game
Dealer East

```
                    ♠ –
                    ♡ 8
                    ◇ K 10 9 4 3
                    ♣ A K Q J 10 8 4
♠ Q 10 9 6 5 3                        ♠ K 4
♡ A 10 6 4 2            N             ♡ K J 9 5 3
◇ 5                  W   E            ◇ A 8
♣ 6                    S              ♣ 9 7 5 3
                    ♠ A J 8 7 2
                    ♡ Q 7
                    ◇ Q J 7 6 2
                    ♣ 2
```

SOUTH	WEST	NORTH	EAST
Dyson	Calderwood	Liggins	Shek
–	–	–	1♡
2♡	4♡	5NT	Pass
6◇	Pass	Pass	Dble
End			

No-one had forced North to bid so high. Even with the vulnerability
in his favour, he surely had some expectation of twelve tricks. It
follows that East's final double should be lead-directional, particularly

as he hadn't doubled 5NT. (Why Shek did double the slam is a mystery. It looks a poor call to me.)

If the double is Lightner, West's best shot is surely to lead a spade, playing for East to be void in that suit. Calderwood preferred to lead his singleton club. Dyson won with dummy's ace and ruffed a club high to reach his hand. When West was unable to overruff, declarer played the ace of spades, disposing of dummy's singleton heart. He could now play on trumps, claiming twelve tricks shortly thereafter. A diamond game was made at the other table, so East–West lost 12 IMPs where they might have gained 11. They eventually lost the final by just 5 IMPs.

Suppose Shek had not doubled the slam. What then? My bet is that West would have found the winning lead of the heart ace.

You are representing Brazil in the 1985 Bermuda Bowl, which is being contested in your own country before a partisan crowd. You have reached the semi-final, against the mighty USA team. What is more, on Board 158 out of 160 you tactically underbid your hand, inducing the great Bob Hamman to double you in Four Spades, made with an overtrick! You feel that your side may be in the lead (in fact you are 6 IMPs ahead). Are you looking for a peaceful and dull penultimate board? No, it will fall to you to try to make a doubled slam! This is the board:

North–South game
Dealer North

♠ A 7 3
♡ 10 8 6 5
♢ Q
♣ A 10 8 3 2

♠ Q 9 5
♡ –
♢ K J 6 2
♣ Q J 9 7 5 4

SOUTH	WEST	NORTH	EAST
M. Branco	Wolff	P. Branco	Hamman
–	–	Pass	1♡
2♣	4♡	5♣	5♡
Pass	Pass	6♣	Pass
Pass	Dble	End	

West leads ♡K. Contrary to all expectation, you have an excellent chance of making the slam. In fact, all you need to do is to pick up the trump suit. You ruff the heart lead and lead the queen of trumps, West producing the 6. Play the right card from dummy and you will reach the Bermuda Bowl final. Which card is it to be?

This was the full deal:

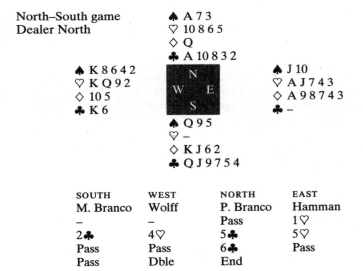

North–South game
Dealer North

```
                    ♠ A 7 3
                    ♡ 10 8 6 5
                    ◇ Q
                    ♣ A 10 8 3 2
♠ K 8 6 4 2                          ♠ J 10
♡ K Q 9 2          N                 ♡ A J 7 4 3
◇ 10 5          W     E               ◇ A 9 8 7 4 3
♣ K 6              S                  ♣ —
                    ♠ Q 9 5
                    ♡ —
                    ◇ K J 6 2
                    ♣ Q J 9 7 5 4
```

SOUTH	WEST	NORTH	EAST
M. Branco	Wolff	P. Branco	Hamman
–	–	Pass	1♡
2♣	4♡	5♣	5♡
Pass	Pass	6♣	Pass
Pass	Dble	End	

The more hearts the Americans bid, the more the Brazilian North liked his hand. He allowed himself to be pushed to Six Clubs and was doubled there. Marcelo Branco ruffed the king of hearts lead and led the trump queen, West producing the 6. A place in the final depended on which card declarer played from dummy.

'Was your partner's pass of Six Clubs forcing?' enquired Branco, seeking an extra clue.

'No,' Wolff replied.

Had it been a forcing pass, this would have strongly indicated first-round control of clubs, the opponents' suit.

The seconds ticked by, then . . . 'Ace!' said Branco.

The slam was one down.

Did you make the same decision? Whether Hamman's pass of Six Clubs was technically forcing or not, it seems very unlikely that he would pass without a void club. North was a passed hand and South had made only a simple non-vulnerable overcall, passing thereafter.

Surely the Brazilians would not be allowed to play there undoubled.
East's pass made sense only if there was some chance that twelve tricks
might be made in hearts.

With the Brazilian East–West pair going one down in Five Hearts at
the other table it was 6 IMPs to the USA instead of 16 to Brazil. The
scores were now level. The Americans gained 3 IMPs on the next
board and went through to the final, where they beat Austria.

It's the last board of the 1996 Olympiad quarter-final, played in
Rhodes. The Austrian and British ladies face each other and a place in
the semi-final will depend on your opening lead here. Sitting West,
with the opponents vulnerable, you hold:

    ♠ 3   ♡ Q 4   ◇ A 9 8 2   ♣ Q J 10 8 6 2

SOUTH	WEST	NORTH	EAST
Pass	3♣	3♠	Pass
3NT	End		

What is it to be? A straightforward queen of clubs or something
more adventurous? This was the deal:

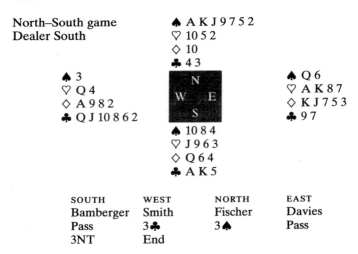

North–South game   ♠ A K J 9 7 5 2
Dealer South   ♡ 10 5 2
                  ◇ 10
                  ♣ 4 3

♠ 3   ♠ Q 6
♡ Q 4   ♡ A K 8 7
◇ A 9 8 2   ◇ K J 7 5 3
♣ Q J 10 8 6 2   ♣ 9 7

                  ♠ 10 8 4
                  ♡ J 9 6 3
                  ◇ Q 6 4
                  ♣ A K 5

SOUTH	WEST	NORTH	EAST
Bamberger	Smith	Fischer	Davies
Pass	3♣	3♠	Pass
3NT	End		

Nicola Smith reached for the club queen and the Austrians made 3NT on a combined total of just 18 points. At the other table Maria Erhart played in 5 ♢ on the West cards, going only 50 down when she guessed the trumps correctly. That was 11 IMPs to Austria and a win by 16 IMPs. Had Smith led ♡Q or a low diamond, 3NT would have gone at least 300 down. That would have given victory to the British team.

Was there any indication that a club lead was not best? For this lead to succeed, you will probably need to find partner with a doubleton club honour. With such a holding is there not a fair chance that she would have bid 4♣ over 3NT, rather than risk a vulnerable game being made on a run of the spade suit? This seems a strong point to me. It is borne out by the actions of Patrick Huang of Taipei, sitting West with the same hand in the Open Olympiad quarter-finals. He passed on the West cards and heard this auction:

SOUTH	WEST	NORTH	EAST
Szymanowski	Huang	Martens	Kuo
Pass	Pass	3♠	Pass
3NT	?		

South had bid 3NT on a passed hand, facing a pre-emptive opening! Rather than risk making the wrong lead, and conceding a huge swing, Huang took out insurance by bidding 4♣ on his own hand. Of course, he knew from the opponents' bidding that East would not hold a bust. The contract went one down, North scoring a diamond ruff. Huang had avoided a big swing, however, and Taipei beat Poland by 10 IMPs.

The 1988 Gold Cup final went to the wire. Plackett, a team of 25-year-olds who had beaten several seeded teams already, faced Breskal, a squad of seasoned internationals. The result turned on this spade game, played by John Collings.

Game all   ♠ K 10 6 5 2
Dealer West   ♡ J 3
                 ◇ K 10 3
                 ♣ K J 4

♠ 7 4   ♠ 9 3
♡ A Q 10 9 7 5   **N**   ♡ 8 6
◇ 7 4   **W**   **E**   ◇ A Q J 9 6 2
♣ 8 5 2   **S**   ♣ Q 9 3

                 ♠ A Q J 8
                 ♡ K 4 2
                 ◇ 8 5
                 ♣ A 10 7 6

SOUTH	WEST	NORTH	EAST
Collings	Dyson	Panto	Bacon
–	2◇ (1)	Pass	Pass
Dble	Pass	3◇	Pass
3♠	Pass	4♠	End

(1) Multi, usually a weak two in a major (6–10 points)

At the other table the defenders had led a diamond and taken the first four tricks – two diamonds and two hearts. If Collings could make the game, his team would win the Gold Cup.

Mindful of partner's pass of the Multi, Dyson also led a diamond. Collings rose with the king, East winning with the ace and cashing the diamond queen. Was it obvious to play a heart now? The young East thought not and played a third diamond.

Collings now had a chance. He ruffed high, drew trumps, then paused to count the defenders' hands. West's shape was known to be 2–6–2–3. So the contract could be made, provided declarer guessed who held ♣Q. Collings asked himself why East had not switched to a heart at trick 3. The most likely explanation, it seemed, was that he held ♡Q and was reluctant to play on the suit in case declarer held the king. And if West held only 4 points in hearts he would need ♣Q to make up the count for his vulnerable weak two. Collings duly finessed West for the club queen, going two down and leaving the youngsters clutching the Gold Cup.

In the final round of the 1993 European Championship Sweden faced old rivals, Norway. They needed a big win to gain Europe's fourth qualifying place for the next Bermuda Bowl. This board, with the Swedes sitting East–West, cost them their trip:

North-South game
Dealer East

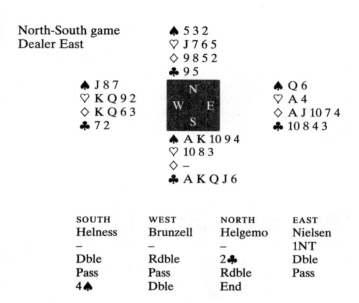

```
                    ♠ 5 3 2
                    ♡ J 7 6 5
                    ◇ 9 8 5 2
                    ♣ 9 5
  ♠ J 8 7               N           ♠ Q 6
  ♡ K Q 9 2        W       E        ♡ A 4
  ◇ K Q 6 3                         ◇ A J 10 7 4
  ♣ 7 2                S            ♣ 10 8 4 3
                    ♠ A K 10 9 4
                    ♡ 10 8 3
                    ◇ –
                    ♣ A K Q J 6
```

SOUTH	WEST	NORTH	EAST
Helness	Brunzell	Helgemo	Nielsen
–	–	–	1NT
Dble	Rdble	2♣	Dble
Pass	Pass	Rdble	Pass
4♠	Dble	End	

At the other table the first two bids had been the same, but 1NT doubled became the final contract – one down. Here the Swedish West redoubled and North bid 2♣, intending to make an SOS redouble on the next round. (This is a dangerous game when vulnerable, because an opponent with a club stack can simply pass and collect a bundle of 100s.)

Would you have passed the redouble of 2♣ on the South cards? I'm sure I would have done. A forcing defence would have held declarer to five trump tricks and ♠A K, so Helness's judgement was superb as he removed the redouble. He bid a full 4♠, since there would be play for this contract when North held as little as a Yarborough with four small trumps.

West doubled and led ♡K. East could have beaten the contract by overtaking and continuing the suit for a heart ruff. Since his doubleton queen of trumps could scarcely contribute to the defence otherwise, this seems the marked defence. East played low at trick 1, however. He won the heart continuation with the ace and switched to a low trump, won by South's ace.

Helness drew a second round of trumps, then continued with the ace, king and jack of clubs. West could have beaten the contract by ruffing with his master trump and cashing a heart. (However, if West does ruff declarer will throw a diamond from dummy. Cashing the heart queen, setting up dummy's jack, would then cost the contract if declarer had started with two hearts and one diamond! If West plays a

diamond instead, dummy's hearts will go on the last two clubs and the
contract will still be made.)

Hoping that his partner held ♣Q – not very likely after South's 4♠ bid
on a 5-card suit – West discarded on the third club instead of ruffing.
Helness threw one of dummy's hearts and continued with the club
queen. Whether or not West ruffed now, declarer would throw dummy's
last heart and make the contract by ruffing a heart in dummy. As a result
Sweden just missed out on the fourth spot for the Chile Bowl. The Dutch
team took their places and . . . went on to become world champions.

The 1993 Bermuda Bowl semi-final between Brazil and Norway was
hotly contested. With one board to play, Brazil led Norway by 9 IMPs.
This fateful board then arose:

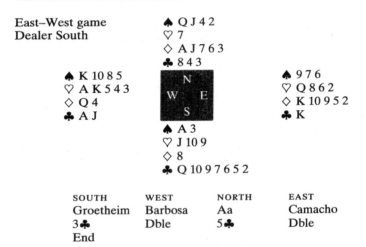

	♠ Q J 4 2	
East–West game	♡ 7	
Dealer South	◇ A J 7 6 3	
	♣ 8 4 3	

♠ K 10 8 5		♠ 9 7 6
♡ A K 5 4 3	N	♡ Q 8 6 2
◇ Q 4	W E	◇ K 10 9 5 2
♣ A J	S	♣ K

	♠ A 3	
	♡ J 10 9	
	◇ 8	
	♣ Q 10 9 7 6 5 2	

SOUTH	WEST	NORTH	EAST
Groetheim	Barbosa	Aa	Camacho
3♣	Dble	5♣	Dble
End			

How many down would you expect? It looks as if declarer will lose
two trumps, one heart and one spade. Two down.

At the other table the bidding had been identical and the Norwegian
defenders had dropped a trick, picking up only 100. In the VuGraph
room the Brazilian supporters were exultant. They were in the final!
Unless – it was impossible of course – the Norwegians should actually
make their doubled club game.

The Brazilian West, Barbosa, led the ace of hearts. When dummy
appeared with a singleton heart, he decided to cut down declarer's
ruffs. He played the ace of trumps and the bare king appeared from his
partner. Ouch! What should West do next? East, who had doubled
5♣, was surely a strong favourite to hold the ace of spades, reasoned
Barbosa. He switched to a spade and Brazil's place in the final was lost.

Dummy's queen won and declarer ruffed two hearts in dummy, using the spade ace and a diamond ruff as entries. Since West still held the spade king, declarer knew it was safe to return to his hand with a spade ruff. He drew the last trump and claimed the contract.

At double-dummy West can lead the jack of trumps, win the heart return, draw a second trump, and force dummy's last trump with a heart. The defenders will score one spade, two hearts and two trumps. Three down! Each of the first three cards played by Barbosa had moved him one trick further from this optimal result.

It seems to me that the key mistake was playing the ace of trumps. There would always be some risk attached to playing a second trump, since declarer might then run the diamond suit. In any case South was unlikely to hold four hearts for his pre-empt, so playing on trumps could save one ruff at best. The best move at trick 2 may be a low diamond. If declarer turns up with the diamond king, East will surely hold the ace of spades.

We'll end the book with a disaster that cost the greatest prize of all – a Bermuda Bowl title. With two boards to go in the 1983 Bowl the Italians led USA by 8 IMPs. Joe Musumeci, the US non-playing captain, had watched the last two boards being played in the Closed Room. 'Two flat games,' was his despondent report. 'There's no way we can pick up 8 IMPs.'

In the VuGraph Room the penultimate board was displayed:

East–West game
Dealer East

		♠ A K J 9 6 2	
		♡ K 7 3	
		◇ K Q 3	
		♣ 8	
♠ 7 4			♠ –
♡ 6	N		♡ Q 10 9 8 2
◇ A J 10 8	W E		◇ 9 7 6 4 2
♣ Q J 7 6 4 3	S		♣ A 9 5
		♠ Q 10 8 5 3	
		♡ A J 5 4	
		◇ 5	
		♣ K 10 2	

SOUTH	WEST	NORTH	EAST
Garozzo	Weichsel	Belladonna	Sontag
–	–	–	Pass
1♠	Pass	2NT	Pass
3♠	Pass	4NT	Pass
5◇	Pass	6♠	End

The Americans quickly cashed two aces and the slam was one down. What on earth had happened? How could two of the world's finest ever bridge players, with Blackwood at their disposal, mistake how many aces they held between them?

The situation was more complex than it might appear. Belladonna's 2NT response agreed spades as trumps and indicated a side-suit singleton somewhere. This response was made on two strengths of hand: game-try and slam-invitational. South was expected to rebid an artificial 3♣, over which North would identify his singleton with 3◇/ 3♡/3♠ (to show a game-try hand) or 3NT/4♣/4◇ (to show a slam-try hand).

Garozzo held such a poor hand that he signed off in 3♠, declining even to ask which singleton partner held. This was an anti-system bid, which Belladonna had not encountered before. Eventually he interpreted it as a trump asking-bid, a convention that they used in various other sequences. Holding six trumps to the ace-king, he made the sixth-step response of 4NT. Garozzo took this as Blackwood and showed one ace. The Italians' wires were now totally crossed. Belladonna read 5◇ as a cue bid, showing a diamond control and denying a club control. Since he held a club control himself, and had not yet shown anything more than a game-try hand, he felt obliged to jump to the slam.

Delving into such a sad hand is rather like attending a funeral. In the cold light of day there was little sense in Belladonna's interpretation of 3♠. If his partner held any type of strong hand he would surely have sought further information with the 3♣ relay. In any case, Garozzo's strength was limited by his failure to open a strong club. He could scarcely be in a position to take control of the bidding, with an asking bid. Interviewed afterwards, Garozzo stated that the auction had been a simple one. 4NT had been Blackwood and Belladonna, one of the greatest players in history, had suffered a mental block on the hand.

News of the sensational deal flashed around the world. Hamman and Wolff stopped in relative safety at the other table (1♠ – 4NT, 5◇ – 5♠) and the Americans gained 11 IMPs. They picked up 2 more on the final board, winning the title by 5 IMPs.

If that board isn't a 'famous bridge disaster', I don't know what is!